More Praise for

Why Did I Get a B?

▪ ▪ ▪ ▪ ▪ ▪ ▪ ▪

"A starkly honest, at times irreverent view of the triumphs and challenges of teaching. Readers will cheer at Reed's accounts of student victories and sigh in exasperation at her descriptions of incompetent administrators. . . . Reed's candid writing about a stressful yet rewarding career will resonate with educators."

—*Library Journal*

"The winning authenticity of educator Shannon Reed's memoir stems from her willingness to explore her strengths and weaknesses as a teacher."

—*Pittsburgh Post-Gazette*

"Divided into comical essays and sincere meditations, *Why Did I Get a B?* provides an accurate depiction of how many teachers feel about their careers. . . . An honest look into how teachers' brains work to solve problems and do what's best for their kids while also just trying to stay alive."

—*BookPage*

"Reflective essays that expose the good and the bad sides of being an educator. Good reading for aspiring teachers."

—*Kirkus Reviews*

"This hilarious, very honest, insightful book is perfect for all the teachers in your life, for the parents who complain about their kids' teachers, and even for the students who don't know how lonely and difficult teaching really is."

—Angie Cruz, professor and author of
Dominicana

"Smart, witty, and sharply observed. I laughed, I cried, I cringed. But make no mistake—Shannon Reed has written a love letter to teachers. Her cheeky winks and snarky eye rolls are always buoyed by the understanding that teachers love what they do. They'd have to ... otherwise they'd never survive the hell we put them through."

—Siobhan Vivian, professor and *New York Times* bestselling author of *The List*

"A hilarious, smart, and painfully honest look at teaching that's also full of heart. Reed isn't afraid to ridicule the most maddening aspects of the profession, or to admit her own missteps, but she writes about her students and colleagues with a warmth and insight that captures the essence of what education should be. *Why Did I Get a B?* somehow made me laugh at all the things that frustrate me most about my work as a teacher, while also reminding me why I love it."

—Anjali Sachdeva, professor and author of
All the Names They Used for God

Why Did I Get a B?

And Other Mysteries We're Discussing in the Faculty Lounge

Shannon Reed

ATRIA PAPERBACK

New York · London · Toronto · Sydney · New Delhi

An Imprint of Simon & Schuster, Inc.
1230 Avenue of the Americas
New York, NY 10020

Copyright © 2020 by Shannon Reed

First Atria Paperback edition June 2021

ATRIA PAPERBACK and colophon are trademarks of Simon & Schuster, Inc.

For information about special discounts for bulk purchases,
please contact Simon & Schuster Special Sales at 1-866-506-1949 or
business@simonandschuster.com.

The Simon & Schuster Speakers Bureau can bring authors to your live event. For more information or to book an event, contact the Simon & Schuster Speakers Bureau at 1-866-248-3049 or visit our website at www.simonspeakers.com.

Interior design by Dana Sloan

Manufactured in the United States of America

1   3   5   7   9   10   8   6   4   2

Library of Congress Cataloging-in-Publication Data

Names: Reed, Shannon, author.
Title: Why did I get a B? : and other mysteries we're discussing in the
faculty lounge / Shannon Reed.
Description: First Atria Books hardcover edition. | New York : Atria Books, 2020.
Identifiers: LCCN 2020000555 (print) | LCCN 2020000556 (ebook) |
ISBN 9781982136093 (hardcover) | ISBN 9781982136109 (ebook)
Subjects: LCSH: Reed, Shannon. | Reed, Shannon—Anecdotes. |
Teachers—United States—Biography. | Teaching—United
States—Anecdotes. | Teaching—United States—Humor.
Classification: LCC LA2317.R397 A3 2020 (print) | LCC LA2317.R397 (ebook) |
DDC 371.20092 [B—dc23
LC record available at https://lccn.loc.gov/2020000555
LC ebook record available at https://lccn.loc.gov/2020000556

ISBN 978-1-9821-3609-3
ISBN 978-1-9821-3619-2 (pbk)
ISBN 978-1-9821-3610-9 (ebook)

*This book is dedicated with much love to
my first and best teacher, my wonderful mom,
Gloria Reed
And in memory of my
other most beloved teachers, my dad, the
Reverend Ronald B. Reed, and my grandmother,
Kathryn Zeger.*

Also, thanks for everything, Roo.

And God has placed in the church first of all
apostles, second prophets, third teachers, then
miracles . . .

—*1 Corinthians 12:28a*

Well, to each his own.

—*me to one of my students*

Yeah. To each his crazy-ass own.

—*my student to me*

Contents

Part II: High School

Part III: College

Part IV: A Few Last Tidbits for the Cool Kids Who Like to Hang Out in My Room after School Is Out

Contents

Author's Note

There are two kinds of writing in this book: humor pieces and essays. The humor, which tends to be shorter and, in theory, snappier, often draws on my career as a teacher and professor but isn't factual. The essays, which do reflect my specific experiences, are correct to the best of my ability. Any errors of fact are mine. I've taught a lot of students over a lot of years, and I may have inadvertently conflated people or events. There are also moments when I've chosen to deliberately combine events or characters, or to shorten a timeline. Generally, I've written about Stella Maris High School as it really was, and changed much about the school I call THSB here, because much of my experience at Stella was good, while much of my time at THSB was not.

Additionally, because I am writing about many people who were minors when the events I'm recounting took place, I've gone out of my way to disguise their identities, changing names, genders, ages, appearances, and other characteristics of individual students who probably didn't think they'd end up in their teacher's book someday. I have also changed the names of some adults. Just to keep you on your toes, I've kept some of the names of adults unaltered, mostly when I thought it would make those people happy to see themselves in this book.

Why Did I Get a B?

Preface:
You Are Not Alone

Once, not that long ago, when I was teaching at THSB, a pretty terrible public high school in South Brooklyn, I experienced what I consider to be the most despairing moment of my professional life (thus far). While it was one of many—very many—moments of despair I would feel as a teacher, and particularly at that school, it remains the most vivid in my mind because of how it changed me.

It was the day of the Winter Holidays Talent Show, which was not the reason for the despair (although, let's be honest, the principal's insistence on singing a dirge-like "Go Tell It on the Mountain" while accompanying himself on the guitar would not lift the soul). I had escorted my extremely high-energy class of freshmen to the building's auditorium, where we would watch their schoolmates perform in front of another school's abandoned homecoming banner, which no one had thought to take down. One of my students was one of the most horrible people I've ever met—I call him Paulie in this book, you'll get to know him in an essay later on—and the three-minute walk from our classroom to the auditorium had been more than enough time for Paulie to cause trouble, verbally abusing his classmates and ricocheting off the walls. I had already had to stop one of his peers from hitting him, even as I wished that someone *would* hit him, and hard.

As often happened, the show did not start at the scheduled time, so our large group of students from the Theatre High School of Brooklyn (hence THSB) grew more and more agitated, stewing in the deepening agony of being forced to sit in uncomfortable chairs, staring at a sign reading GET DOWN WITH COLLEGE PREP HIGH SCHOOL, waiting for this stupid event the grown-ups had forced them to attend to be over so that they could be done with school and be out into their real lives already. Paulie was seated near a young man called Marvin, a thin, gangly kid in a striped polo buttoned to the neck, whom I always described as "delicate" to myself. He was a frequent target of Paulie's harrassment, and as the waiting dragged on, Paulie started teasing Marvin, drawing the snickers of the bored students around them. Marvin told him to stop, so Paulie imitated Marvin, and Marvin wasn't able to just go still, leaving Paulie with no material to work with, instead getting more and more agitated himself. I was equally annoyed by both of them, the kind of mind-set that's wildly unfair yet not all that uncommon in exhausted teachers. I told Paulie to stop. He didn't. Marvin looked increasingly frantic. I tried to separate them, but Paulie wouldn't move, recognizing that he'd lose the source of the attention he was getting from other students. So I sat down between them, trying to help Marvin and keep this from turning into a Thing that an administrator could yell at me about later. After a moment between them, Paulie crinkled his nose. "You smell," he said to me. "You smell bad."

And get this: Marvin laughed. At me.

He must have been so relieved to have Paulie's fusillade of torment turned on someone else, but oh, how that laughter hurt. It felt like a betrayal. Worn down by many long months of trying to reach Paulie and his classmates, I did what I had so often done when pushed to my emotional limit as a still-newish adult: I burst into hot, angry tears.

Everyone has sensitive spots, and one of mine is being told I smell, so my consternation was genuine, but my sobbing ineffective. No one came to help me—I realize now that all of the other teachers were at least as tired and overworked and focused on their own problems as I was and honestly, what the hell was taking so long? It was a school talent show, not the Moulin Rouge! Marvin and Paulie, now united, giggled together, pointing at me, holding their noses.

So I got up and walked away. And by "away," I mean I abandoned the class. I walked out of the auditorium, up the stairs, back into my classroom, went behind my desk, and collapsed onto the floor, where I sobbed, staring at the mouse droppings underneath the radiator. And still no one came to help me. Through the pipes I could faintly hear "Go Tell It on the Mountain," or imagined I could, and it was the perfect soundtrack for my utter self-pity and genuine despair.

I stayed like that on the floor, moving from sobbing, *SOBBING*, into mere weeping, for about forty-five minutes, until another teacher (who weirdly kept a desk in my classroom, for reasons too stupid to explain) appeared, threw herself into her desk chair, dropped her head into her hands, and began to wail about something awful that had happened to her at the talent show too. She knew I was there. I knew she was there. But we both just stayed in our own corners, crying.

That was it: the most sunk moment of my teaching life. I could see that she needed help, but I had no help to give. I also needed help, but didn't expect her to provide it. I could see no way forward in working with those kids. I expected to be fired since I had effectively walked off the job, and it was likely that Paulie had killed Marvin while I was gone. The only truly helpful quality I had as a teacher of those very, very difficult students was that I really, really cared about them, and yet I had abandoned them. I hated them for being mean, I hated myself for being weak, and I hated my colleague for not being a wizened old noble teacher who could pat my head and give me good advice. I hated "Go Tell It on the Mountain." I had never been more alone in my entire life.

It occurs to me now that perhaps my colleague, Marvin, and even Paulie felt exactly the same way.

———

Let's fast-forward, shall we? In the short term, no one even noticed that I had left the auditorium, which tells you a lot about that school. I wasn't fired, and when I called the teachers' union hotline to ask what I should do, the woman who answered said, "Well, I wouldn't bring up that you left, to start with." So when the kids returned to the classroom to grab their stuff, I didn't say a word except "See you tomorrow!" and they cheerfully bid me goodbye as they always did—or at least the ones who bothered to talk to me did. No administrator ever disciplined me.

But it also worked out for me in the end. I mean not immediately it didn't, I hated that job, and I struggled for three more years to get out of it, and my colleague turned out to be super odd, and that principal's fondness for inappropriately religious material ended up being the best thing about him. But these days, I have a pretty great job, still teaching, and I'm much happier, and my students *never* tell me I smell.

Of course, in that moment, I knew none of the future ahead of me. I've never forgotten how utterly abandoned I felt, or how impossible it was to reach out of my own despair and look after someone else. I hope that most readers of this book have not had such terrible days in the classroom, but I bet you still know exactly what it was like, because to be a good teacher is to care very much about people, which is an effective way to get your heart thoroughly broken on the regular.

There's just a little bit more to that story, by the way. I went home and told my best friend, Andrew, about what had happened. At first, of course, he was all sympathy and concern, but, as often happens with us, we were soon laughing.

"Why did you run away and lie on the floor and stare at the heater?" he asked.

"I don't know," I said. "I guess maybe I hoped that a teacher on the floor above or below me would hear me, and send a message through the pipes . . ."

"Like in a prison movie! You tried to *Shawshank* it!"

"I totally did!"

As we laughed, I realized what had changed for me in those moments of despair: I had grown up. Not completely (as if), but I was wiser than I had been at the start of the day, when I was aggrieved and aggravated by Paulie and his classmates, who insisted on behaving badly no matter what I did. The challenges that Paulie and Marvin faced (some self-generated) were much greater than anything I had ever dealt with. They were going to continue to be cruel to me, I realized, and I was going to take it, because they needed me (or *someone*, and I was the lucky winner) quite a lot. That was the work I had to do, and I expected—rightly—to fail at it mostly, and very occasionally succeed.

But the loneliness I had felt and had seen in my crying colleague, well, that was something I could fix right away. I could joke, tease, cajole, and laugh with my students and my colleagues. My sense of humor is who I am, one of my deepest resources to call upon. No student, no teacher, ever had to feel alone like that so long as I could say or write something to prove that they were not, often in the form of a very sarcastic joke.

Dear readers, I hope that this book is a message through the pipes for you: you are not alone in the difficult and beautiful work of teaching, of caring for others, of being alive. There is much to share, and worry over, and laugh about.

Have a seat. Class is in session.

Do You Have What It Takes to Be a Teacher?: A Quiz

1. You are at a baseball game, and there are several little boys seated behind you loudly making fart noises instead of watching the game. Do you . . .
    a. Ignore them?
    b. Glare at the adults with them but do nothing?
    c. Turn around, tell them to stop, bond with them over a discussion about the infield fly rule, get them to teach you how to do that armpit thing, and part ways at the end of the game with hugs and one last fart noise?

2. The fire alarm in your hotel is going off. Do you . . .
    a. Roll over and go back to sleep. It's probably nothing?
    b. Call the front desk to complain?
    c. Make sure everyone on your floor is out, sort them into groups by room, and ask everyone to share what brings them to Peoria while you wait for the fire company?

3. Who is your favorite fictional teacher?
    a. The teacher in Van Halen's "Hot for Teacher" video.

7

  b. I've never noticed any fictional teachers. I enjoy *Modern Family*, though.

  c. Anne Shirley, Jane Eyre, literally any other fictional teacher except the teacher in Van Halen's "Hot for Teacher" video.

4. You have been taking this quiz for three questions. Have you . . .

  a. Started playing on your phone yet?

  b. Already begun composing a firmly worded letter to the publisher about how quizzes are too challenging to be included in a book that children might read?

  c. Figured out that you should always guess C because those answers are what teachers would do?

5. Okay, then, so why are you still taking this quiz?

  a. Am I? I'm mostly playing *Candy Crush* at this point.

  b. I'm gathering material for my firmly worded letter.

  c. Teachers value working to completion, even if they've already figured out what's what.

If you answered mostly As, you should look into becoming a school administrator.

—

If you answered mostly Bs, you are a parent who will drive at least one teacher nuts.

—

If you answered mostly Cs, you definitely have what it takes to be a teacher.

If People Talked to Other Professionals the Way They Talk to Teachers

- "Ah, a zookeeper. So, you just babysit the animals all day?"
- "My colon never acts this way at home. Are you sure you're reading the colonoscopy results correctly? Did you ever think that maybe you just don't like my colon?"
- "I'd love to just play with actuary statistics all day. That would be so fun! I bet you don't even feel like you're at work!"
- "You're a sanitation worker, huh? I hated my garbage collectors when I was growing up. One of them once yelled at me when I stood directly in front of their truck and kept it from completing its appointed rounds, and ever since then I've just loathed all of them, everywhere."
- "So you run a ski lodge? Do you just, like, chill during the summer? Must be nice."
- "Since my singer-songwriter thing isn't taking off yet, I've been thinking about going into lawyer-ing. I mean, how hard

can it be? I know criminals tend to like me, or at least the two that I see once a year at Thanksgiving do."

- "I bet that's the best part of being a banker—all the free money!"

- "Do you even read your patients' charts, or do you just assign them a random dosage based on how nice they've been to you?"

- "Before you give me a ticket, Officer, I just wanted to mention: my taxes pay your salary."

- "Excuse me, my seven-year-old son, who mere minutes ago lied about whether he had to pee or not, just told me that you wouldn't give him any ketchup even though he says he asked for it politely. Now I'm going to ask the manager to move us to another server's table, and also fire you."

- "Since you're a plumber, and you're around them all day, I have to ask—do you ever find one of your pipes attractive? Even though you know you shouldn't go there?"

- "Sure, the pay is low, but I bet the joy of putting together press releases for local events is reason enough to stick with this job in the events division of the chamber of commerce. You must really believe in its mission."

- "Oh, you're a stand-up comedian, huh? So, you just stand up there and bullshit until your set is done?"

- "Damn! Look at you in that dress! Now I'm Hot for Quality Control Manager for the Western Division!"

Part I

Preschool, Elementary School, and Middle School

How I Came to Teach Preschool

When I was growing up, people often asked me if I intended to be a pastor (as my father and his dad were) or a teacher (as my mom had been and her mom was). Despite the question, it was clear that everyone thought I was on my way to clergy-dom. I liked to be center stage, and pastors often are. Teachers, everyone knew, ceded the spotlight to their students, fading away to let others shine, but I took the instructions of "This Little Light of Mine" very seriously: I was gonna let it *shine*. That meant being a pastor.

My family seemed to agree with my instincts, knowing my fondness for drama and high emotion, which, let's face it, come in handy at Easter. They also knew my short temper, which perpetually ended up serving me poorly in any kind of academic setting. And while no one exactly said it, with my sarcasm and healthy sense of skepticism, I sure didn't seem to be the sweet and nurturing type. My mom's mom, my Mum-mum, was an excellent veteran teacher who never strongly encouraged me to be one when I was a child. Instead, she made sure I knew it was very hard work. I didn't mind working hard, but I wanted everyone to know I was.

I grew up in a happily religious family that believed we were each called to do something with our lives; my father often talked about feeling called to serve God as a pastor. The expectation that I would be called to something too was strong for me. Back then, I thought of being called as very dramatic, like those Bible stories where shrubbery bursts into flames and messages are clearly enunciated from heaven. Nothing like that happened to me, certainly never about my career options. Eventually, I started to realize that I felt whatever the opposite of being called was about being a pastor. I could almost hear God saying, "Thanks, but pass." But I still didn't want to teach.

Honestly, I just thought being a teacher was so . . . *typical*. In the mid-1990s in Western Pennsylvania, it was almost a de facto career for a young woman who didn't want to be a nurse or a stay-at-home mom. When I decided to get my undergraduate degree in theatre, most everyone told me it would be a great credential for a teacher to hold. Even after I managed to convince everyone I was not going to be a pastor, they still urged teaching on me. The family business and a reliable one at that! I could do it until I got married! I'd have summers off to do my theatre stuff!

But I couldn't picture myself as a teacher. Setting aside my family, there were only two kinds in my limited educational experience: first, terrible teachers, who had checked out twenty years before retirement and were just going through the motions. I knew I could not be that kind of teacher, ever. They had ruined too much of my formal education for me. The other kind of teachers were martyrs who gave up everything for "their" kids, like the high school teacher I had who worked at the school from 6 A.M. until 6 P.M. every day. I couldn't do that either. I wanted to have a full, rich, interesting life, with travel and friends and books and love. I didn't want to spend my life working to glorify other people's annoying kids. I was entering adulthood not long after *Mr. Holland's Opus* was released, which summed up everything I disliked about teaching. I mean, come on, it's a movie that ends with a gifted artist, who's been ignored as a composer for decades while he helped mostly untalented students learn to play instruments they would abandon once they graduated, finally having his work performed by an amateur orchestra. Then he promptly retires/heads off into the dying of the light. I was not going to be a Mr. Holland.

I often tell my worried college students that much of their first few years after graduation will be the strange meeting of what they thought they would do in adulthood and what they are actually doing—and what they are learning they want to do. I should know—that's exactly what happened to me. After a brief false start as a reporter for a local radio station, which lasted just long enough for me to realize I hate asking crying strangers whose house has just burned down how to spell their last name, I moved back in with my parents and younger brother in Johnstown, Pennsylvania, and started looking for work. A small town in Western Pennsylvania is a terrible venue for the young job-hunter, especially one with a BFA in Theatre, but it turned out that there was a job I was qualified for: I could be the opener at Richland Learning Center, the preschool and day care center in the basement of my father's church, a large-ish complex on top of a hill with a great view of the Allegheny Mountains and the valley where the city of Johnstown nestles.

Hello, nepotism much? Yep. It's still a little embarrassing, twenty years later, that I had to get a job this way. On the other hand, there was not a ton of competition for it. I was required to be at the RLC at 5:45 A.M. Parents started dropping their kids off at six o'clock, since a lot of them worked the early shifts at the steel mills and hospitals downtown. Reliable early risers with clearances to work with children are not a dime a dozen, even in an economically depressed town. And let's not overlook the fact that I had some relevant experience. While my deep knowledge of the production history of *Pippin* wasn't particularly helpful, after four summers of working at two sleep-away camps, I understood the demands of working with children. I grasped basic concepts like you can't hit them, and you can't let them wander off. It's true that I never would have taken the job at the RLC without absolutely needing to, and I doubt they would have hired me if they hadn't absolutely had to. But I had to, and they did too.

I very nearly didn't get a chance to prove that I'm reliable. I overslept the first morning I was to arise at 5 A.M. My mother woke me in a panic at 5:25, and I was in my car within fifteen minutes making the five-minute trip to the church. I never overslept again (and my mom, proving that she's the best, got up before me *every* day to cook me a hot breakfast).

Getting up insanely early is a necessary evil in many teachers' lives, and while I've never taken to it, I did learn to enjoy the sunrise. That route out of my parents' driveway, past the restaurant where my brother and sister-in-law's wedding reception would be held in a few years, past the coffee shop where the food would be bland enough for my dad when he was sick two decades later, past the hair salon where my mom and I went for manicures sometimes, within sight of the graveyard where a friend of mine from high school was buried, with just a glimpse of the tiny community library where I had held my first job as a library page ($3 per hour) before I turned into the church's parking lot, was and is a special one to me. On a very clear day, off in the distance, I could spot the orderly green farms of Somerset County as well as the paths through pine forests on the mountains that marked the runs of our nearest ski resort. The sun cracked open in the sky over the Alleghenies and the city, spilling gold and blue and pink. By the time I creaked open the old wooden door and walked past my dad's office to the basement, I was awake and ready to distribute hugs and high fives.

Yet I still wasn't really a teacher. "Child Supervisor/Entertainer" is a better term for what I did, or perhaps "Professional Decent Adult." I was not excellent at the job—I had favorites among the kids and a propensity for screeching when things veered toward chaos. When pressed, I defaulted to responding exactly as my mom would have, usually with a sharply worded "Boys and girls!"

Luckily for me, my mom is a great educator, so imitating her was a good choice. Despite my flaws, I was beginning to show signs of who I would become as a teacher, and where my strengths would lie: I liked to organize the day clearly. I was principally concerned with the quality of my students' experiences. I was firm, but loving. I told the truth to parents and students alike. I laughed an awful lot with my kids.

Because the RLC was both a day care and a preschool, we had a wide variety of students, and an ever-shifting population. Almost everyone was dropped off before seven. The preschoolers were handed off to their teachers around seven thirty. In the meantime, various buses arrived to fetch various kids to various schools; most went to the same district I had attended, but there were quite a few private elementary schools in Johnstown too. After everyone was safely on their way, I'd walk around the day care rooms flipping lights off and drift by the other rooms in the basement, where preschoolers were playing, singing, or eating, their sweet, high voices echoing along the linoleum-lined hallway. Church basements have a unique smell—a mix of flop sweat, cooked ham, candle wax, and wine—and there, a layer of baby powder and mud was mixed in. It smelled almost holy.

Then I'd head home for a nap and lunch—again, provided by my wonderful mother, whom you can already tell is the real MVP of

Shannon Reed

my teaching career—before going back to collect the preschoolers. Their school day ended around three but many wouldn't be picked up until much later. I'd also welcome the elementary kids off the buses and get everyone a snack, then provide a structured environment for homework, sports, and so on before handing everyone off to the right adult by dinnertime. The older kids were technically my responsibility, but there were fewer and fewer of them as the afternoons wore on, since they were off to lessons, practices, confirmation classes, and other activities.

I therefore started spending a lot of time with the preschoolers who were left. That I liked this was a surprise to me, as I'd never really spent much time with kids that young. Turns out, though, that preschoolers are my jam.

Why? I don't know if you've heard about this, but preschoolers are pretty cute. Even the cranky, spoiled ones—cute. They say funny things. They giggle a lot. They fall down in comedic ways. They're terrible at sports. They like to read books and sing songs. You can see expressions move across their faces like waves on the ocean. They're often off in their own worlds. These are all qualities that I share. BFFs forever!

Also, they're pretty cuddly. By the end of the day, I was often to be found sitting on the floor of the church's gym, watching a couple of third graders "play" "basketball" while several three- or four-year-olds sat in or near my lap and sang "Itsy Bitsy Teeny Weenie Tiny Little Froggy." It was nice. I had just spent four years in the cutthroat competitive environment of a college theatre program, one in which I almost never excelled. And I had gotten up at 5 A.M. I needed some cuddling, and for someone to love hearing me sing. Like the Grinch, my heart grew three sizes every time one of the kids said, *"Again,* Miss Shannon!"

I have a very specific memory of stopping to talk to my dad in the hallway on my way to the gym one day, making me just a tiny bit later than usual—no big deal, there was another adult in the gym, and we ran a loose ship in general—but when I finally went in, I saw five or six tiny faces looking worriedly at the door. Upon spotting me, they were thrilled—like, absolutely thrilled. There was clapping! There were squeals of delight! MacKenzie ran to give me a hug! Miss Shannon, who they'd seen literally five minutes ago, had returned! It's hard not to love being loved like that.

Since this was in the days before we went to the internet with our every query, I started taking home the magazines for preschool teachers that were around and reading up on how to best work with little kids. My mom and grandmother gave me many of their old teaching resources and answered my questions about how to teach letters and numbers. I learned how to offer two choices instead of asking, "What do you want to sing?" I started using sentences like "Time out!" and "Ow! That hurts my body!" and "Do you need to toilet?" I brought in books from the library that went with the theme of the week (in preschool there is always a Theme of the Week, and I'll note that adult life is better when you have a Theme of the Week too), and read them to the kids. When they developed a devoted fondness for one of those library books, I bought it at the bookstore in the mall so we could keep reading it. Honestly, maybe I was happy that there was a group of people whom I liked and who thought I was rocking Being an Adult. Whatever it was, I wanted in.

———

The preschool ended for the summer, and the preschool teachers had priority for the seasonal work that remained at the RLC, so I was out of a job for a few months. That worked out just fine for me, as I was going back to Camp Ballibay in northeastern Pennsylvania to co-direct the Girls' Division and direct a couple of plays. But before I left, the director of the RLC called me into her office and asked if I wanted to teach preschool the following year. I wouldn't be the head teacher—without a teaching degree, I couldn't hold that title. They couldn't pay me much (I ended up clearing less than $20,000, the first time I realized how underpaid teachers are), but I wouldn't have to get up at 5 A.M., and I would spend every day with those cuddle-bugs. I was a little worried because I had no real idea what a preschool curriculum should look like or how the kids would best be taught, but the director said it was fine, as the head teacher would take care of all of that. My job would be to sing with the kids, read them stories, help them with difficulties (that was code for "clean them up after they wet their pants"), talk to parents at pickup, and stuff like that. It was a great opportunity, especially in the context that I had no other opportunities.

Of course I said yes, and went off to camp genuinely excited about the next fall, and even a little excited about the next stage in Being an Adult after that. Agreeing to become a preschool teacher didn't seem like a profound life choice. It seemed like the next thing, another role to play in the play called *Being Shannon*.

Later that summer, I was sitting on the stage of one of the many outdoor theatres at Ballibay, watching the sunset through the trees and talking to a camper I'd known for a few years. We started discussing what was next, after the camp season wrapped up. She was going on to her senior year at a posh Manhattan high school. I told her I was going to teach preschool.

"But," she said, wrinkling her nose, "I thought you didn't want to be a teacher. You always say that."

"Oh, yeah," I said. "I don't. This is a temporary thing. I'm going to apply to grad school." This was a plan I had concocted recently, and I liked saying those words, which sounded extremely Adult.

"Oh? In what?" she asked.

". . . Educational Theatre."

A beat.

I rushed to add ". . . at NYU!" hoping that my prospective move to Manhattan would distract her from my intended major. But her look told me that she was well aware of what people with a master's in Educational Theatre did: become teachers. I didn't mention to her that I planned to enroll as a double major, earning my certificate to teach secondary English, too. After all, that was just a backup so I could teach while I figured out what I really wanted to do. She continued to arch an eyebrow at me. I turned the conversation to a less fraught topic.

———

The shift in my understanding of who I was going to be had begun, but it wasn't until the fall of my first year of teaching preschool that it was complete. I remember the moment perfectly: I was outside with my class on one of the last warm days in September. Western Pennsylvania tends to slowly sink into seasons rather than abruptly shift from one to the next, which meant that we could admire the leaves just beginning to change on the oak and maple trees around the church property while the weakening sun still kept it warm enough to be outside without coats.

I no longer remember exactly what I was saying about the change of seasons, but the gist was that I was running through the basics of fall, how more leaves would change color and then *fall* to the ground, and that a new season, also *fall*, was beginning. It hadn't yet occurred to me that I was not reminding these preschoolers of exceedingly well-known facts but rather teaching them something they did not already know (RED ALERT: The leaves will fall off the trees!). I'd soon learn that being the first provider of basic information about life is one of the great pleasures of teaching preschoolers.

I picked up a large maple leaf and let it go above my head. We watched it float to the ground. "See," I said. "*Fall.* It fell."

Nick was a sweetheart, big on hugs and short on crying. The best thing about him was that he had a wide-open face, the kind that allowed whatever he was feeling to play across it. As I dropped the leaf and said "Fall," I saw his huge brown eyes grow two sizes like a cartoon character's, and his jaw actually dropped.

"Ohhhhh," Nick said. "I *get* it." He picked up a leaf of his own and turned to the kid next to him. "Milos!" he said. "*Fall!*" He dropped it. "*It fell!*" Milos blinked twice, then smiled. He got it too.

That was it for me, the first moment I was ready to admit I was no longer just a person who liked kids and liked that they liked me. No. I was a teacher. I had *taught.* They had *learned.* They were smarter now! I was hooked.

In that moment, I instinctively understood that I was going to have to follow that old theatre motto: hold on tightly, let go loosely. I had held on to my belief for years that I was not, could not be, a teacher. My reasons were good, and, as it would turn out, justified. I've spent my entire career fighting for what's best for my students, but also fighting for the right to be myself. I mean, I control my temper these days, but I've never given up on being skeptical or sardonic.

But I knew then, at twenty-three, it was time to be honest: I already had been working with kids for years, and I was, at that very moment, teaching. I was becoming a teacher, even if I assured myself that it was just the thing I would do as well as I could until whatever I was supposed to be became clear. A lot of my friends were in or heading to New York, working one-off and temp jobs while they auditioned and waited for their acting careers to start. But I knew that as right as that was for them, it was wrong for me: I had to do something that was meaningful for me every day, not just put in the time until my life started. Who knew when that would be, anyway? And here I had a job full of meaning and wonder and glitter and pumpkins and naps and books. I should embrace it. So I did.

Despite that shift, I still believed that my calling would feel like being tapped on the shoulder by God. It would take me several years to realize that a calling can become clear in the doing. It's what I feel when I write something that's really funny, that I know is going to bring people joy (and possibly tell truth to power). Or when my class at the University of Pittsburgh has a vigorous discussion of *Lincoln in the Bardo* and everyone leaves excited about the possibilities of fiction. Or in the peace that came over me when I sat on the preschool's cheap carpet, a Lego poking into my butt, rubbing two little backs so two little people would fall asleep during naptime.

So I'd be a teacher, on my own terms. There had to be ground rules. First, I let go of that silly concern, the fear of following in a parent's footsteps too closely. Who cared? (Answer: Literally no one cared, except for those people, like my parents and grandparents, who were delighted. Mum-mum was thrilled, and the memory of her pride still fills me with gratitude and love.)

I also decided that I would never work eighty hours a week (a vow I have mostly kept, give or take an intense week here and there) and that I wouldn't be a martyr to my job, which I have also managed despite immense pressure. I vowed I would have a full, rich life, and keep my sense of humor, and be a little edgy. I promised myself that I would stay me, even if I didn't always know who that me was going to be. (Eventually, I would find that there are plenty of other fun, cool, hip, lovely teachers who've stayed themselves too.)

And I promised myself that whenever I could remember to do it, I'd put my students first in our classroom.

And then, just like that, I was a teacher.

Other Vehicular Styles
of Parenting

Push Scooter Parents
Begin the day with extremely high expectations for their children but by 8 P.M. have reduced their rules to "It would be great if you don't smear mayonnaise on the iPad."

Subaru Outback Parents
Regardless of sexual orientation, have a copy of *Heather Has Two Mommies* in their child's library on principle.

Hummer Parents
Chiefly concerned with making their presence known at school events, often arriving late and entering noisily during the principal's welcome speech, then standing at the front of the auditorium to take photos of their children during the concert.

Motorcycle Parents
Never pick their child up on time, most of their conversation is about getting a tattoo, constantly bring up the last scene of *The Breakfast Club* at school events.

Submarine Parents

Plead that they are too busy with work to attend school events, then suddenly emerge at their child's birthday party to charm everyone.

Combine Harvester Parents

Pass out business cards and coupons at Back to School Night, give their kid Avon catalogs to hand out to teachers.

Mobile Home Parents

Always have a large variety of healthy snacks and a change of clothes available; chief organizers of the apple-picking field trip car pool.

Tractor Parents

Drag along one or more recalcitrant younger children to their oldest child's sporting events, dropping shoes/pacifiers/Cheerios on their way.

Eighteen-Wheeler Parents

Older parents in poor shape who fail to see others trying to pass them on the walk up the hill to the pool, track, or football field.

Schooner Parents

Seize upon the most positive note on their child's report card ("very outgoing") and ignore the lurking trouble below ("but incapable of focusing for more than ten seconds").

Yacht Parents

Only see their children at the annual Christmas card photo shoot.

Blimp Parents

Only vaguely aware of their children's activities ("Jessica plays . . . soccer? Softball? Tennis?"), which they hear about at night from their spouse's half-asleep recitation of the day's events.

747 Parents

Often late to PTA meetings without any real explanation but can be counted on to bring the beverages.

Space Shuttle Parents

Sign their kids up for a variety of ambitious activities (Lego camp, piano lessons, Boy Scouts) but only rarely get them to them on time, often, or at all.

All Your Children
Are Broken

I eventually taught at another preschool after finishing my master's in Educational Theatre and English Secondary Teaching at NYU, after being a student teacher in Queens, after a couple of years in publishing. It was an expensive school in Manhattan, and though I loved my students and liked some of my colleagues, it was an unhappy place, caught in a constant tension between demanding, wealthy parents and a weak administration without a clear vision. Given the extraordinarily high cost of tuition, the administration wanted, above all, to keep the parents happy. Unfortunately, that often involved telling parents that their kids were perfect in every way.

No kid is perfect, though. As the teachers of the youngest children, my co-teachers and I were often the first people to spot potential issues in our students—a hearing or vision impairment, early signs of processing disorders, indications that a child might be on the autism spectrum. Understandably, few parents take news that their child might have a medical condition or disability well; anxious, entitled parents sometimes took such news very badly indeed when we tried to gently break it to them. I started to call these awkward, unhappy conversations the Your Child Is Broken Talks to myself. They almost never went well. The administration always took the side—as if it made any sense to even have sides!—of the parents, and as the dust settled with another child not getting the support they needed, that can kicked down the road until they were in a school with an administration that really cared about them, I'd daydream about a different world.

———

If I ran a preschool—ha!—but if I did, I'd start by gathering all of the parents together one fine fall morning. I'd have photos of every child in the class posted on the room's walls, and I'd ask the parents to walk around and look at them, seeing how beautiful they are. "Really look at them," I'd say. "That smile, those eyes, that spark." After that, we'd sit in a circle and I'd give every parent time to describe their child: his emotions, her talents, the way he lifts his head when he hears a bird's song outside, how she names and keeps a rock from every trip she's made to the beach, their habit of blinking instead of winking, the way they tug on their ear as they fall asleep.

This might take hours of listening. It wouldn't matter. In my preschool, there are no pressing obligations, and we have snacks and potty breaks just like the kids. The chairs are comfortable. Our phones don't work except to show relevant photographs, and best of all, we don't mind. Our capacity to listen to the lovely qualities of the children is limitless.

When all has been said and every child praised, and perhaps after we all have some cake in a flavor we like very much, I'd quietly get to my feet, my face wet with tears from so much gorgeousness, so much love. And then I'd remind the gathered parents that their children are beautiful, yes, but also broken. That being human is being broken. I'd paraphrase the great Leonard Cohen to them: the cracks are where the light gets in. "Don't you want your children to be made of light?" I'd say, and in my preschool this sounds profound, not like the ranting of a cult leader.

There'd be rustling, a whisper of "Yes, but my child isn't broken! She can be of the light anyway!" running through the room. "Oh, no," I'd say with the firmness and affection of Emma Thompson correcting a child who's pulled her hair. "No. I'm sorry, it's scary, I know, but yes, really, they are broken. They are human, and to be human is to be broken."

I'd tell the parents that I taught a child who didn't have an upper lip, and one with a misshapen head. Several who needed glasses before they were two. A child who could only say "ball" long, long, long after we thought she'd pick up more words. That I taught a child who couldn't swallow correctly. That there was another who had no hair. And another with a catheter from eight months old on.

Look around us, I'd say, pointing at my staff. I was a child who couldn't hear well. My co-teacher, a person of color, is frequently asked "Where are you from?" and not in a nice way. Our head classroom teacher, another person of color, is always assumed to be the assistant. Another teacher in the school always wears long sleeves to cover his scars. Another doesn't want to go home because she'll be hit. Another waits to leave work until rush hour is over so she'll be sure to get a seat on the train to rest her aching legs.

These children are broken, I'd say, but that doesn't mean they aren't loved. They are too fat and too thin and have weak bones or too-strong bones and have lisps that make "start" sound like "fart." They don't know how to use the potty yet, as they approach five years on Earth. They bite their fingers until they bleed. They twist their hair until it falls out. They can't run too fast because of their hearts. They need a chair all the time. They can't go out in the sun.

They get too angry too quickly. Noises are too much for them. And on. And on. And on.

"See?" I'd say. "We are all very broken, and we will talk about your child's brokenness at preschool this year, not as an accusation—for how can we accuse or hate someone for being what we are ourselves? No," I'd say, "it's a gift to be told your child's uniqueness, because we will love your children more than anyone who isn't their family has so far. We will love them almost as much as you do, although we will keep our commentary about this love more concise than you did. We will not heal the brokenness, but we will fill it with light."

And then I'd open the door to the massive yard my preschool would have and we'd be able to see the children already out there, waiting. Then I'd say, let's go tell them how much we love them. Let's all of us take our brokenness outside and play.

It's Cooking Day at Preschool!

Okay, everyone, let's crisscross applesauce our legs and put our hands in our laps—Jakey, hands in your, no, Jakey, in *your* lap, not Henry's lap, Henry gets to decide whose hands go in his lap. Okay! Great! So, can anyone tell the class the name of the special room we're in? Sorry, what was that, Harper? Uh, no, we're not in the basilica. That's a big word, though; good for you! Anyone else? That's right, Gertrude! We're in a kitchen! So, can anyone guess *why* we're in the kitchen? It has to do with what we've been talking about all week! Does anyone—Jacob! Hands in your own lap!—does anyone remember—JACOB. Do I need to get the *stickers*? Thank you, Jakey, that's better—so, does anyone remember what we're studying this week? No, sorry, Harper, it's not basilicas. Dylan S.? Yes, that's right, *bread*. Today we're going to make some bread, because it's Thursday, and for some godforsaken reason we've decided to make Thursday Cooking Day this year.

What kind of bread, Panacea? That's a great question! Can we all snap for Panacea for asking a gre— Jakey, please come back and sit down. Jakey! Crisscross applesauce! JACOB. Thank you, Jakey.

Wait, Henry, where are you going? Why are you crying, honey? Oh, you're scared of *bread*? That's not what I was expecting. Could you tell Ms. Natalie why? Because you saw your papa punch bread dough one time? Oh dear, that does sound upsetting. But there's seriously no way I'm going to try to make bread dough with all y'all, so don't worry! No punching! Come on back! Thank you, Henry. Snaps for Henry and Panacea.

Class, we're going to use a bread maker! Now, Miss Lara, she said that using a bread maker is kind of cheating, but I don't think it is! I think Miss Lara should mind her own business! Here's the bread maker; you can see it's heavy and very white, very pretty. Which is not to imply that things that are white are prettier than other things, uh, anyway!

Would you like to touch it? Okay, one at a time, you can stand up and walk over and touch it. Carlise, you first. Panacea? Melody-lynn? Dylan S.? Dylan P.? Dylan S.-P.? Great, I love how you're taking turns! Henry, how about you? Okay, yes, you and Jakey can touch it together. Oh, that was great, that was very brave. Jakey! Why did you punch the bread maker? Oh, I see, you were protecting Henry. Hmm, that seems both well intentioned and difficult to allow. Since there are no other adults in the room because Mr. Kenny called in sick again today, I'm going to let it go. Did everyone get to touch the bread maker? What was that, Harper? Uh-huh. Uh-huh. Uh-huh. Uh-huh. Uh-huh. Jakey, stop! Uh-huh. Uh-huh. Okay! Well, I didn't know all that about flying buttresses. Thanks, Harper! Snaps for Harper, whose dads must have bought her a book about church architecture, everyone.

Here's a box of the ingredients we'll need to make bread with my bread maker. There's flour, baking powder, sugar, and yeast. Can anyone guess what the last ingredient I'll need is? It's in this kitchen. What do you think, Dylan S.? Awww, love is very important! That's true! I should always cook with love. But I was thinking of something a little more practical.

Nope, it's not chocolate chips, Morgan, although I'm sure they would be very good in bread.

Nope, it's not strawberries either, but that's a good guess, Panacea, you're on fire today.

Not real fire, Henry, it's an expression.

What? Frogs? No, Alithia! Not frogs, gross.

Henry, please come back, I promise that we won't put frogs in our bread. *I promise.*

Water! The last ingredient we need is water! Water is very important! Remember when our theme of the week was water and we went to the water park, and we had a water-balloon battle, and we painted with watercolors? Really? No one remembers that? It was literally last month. Wow. Okay. Well, anyway, it's water.

Who would like to measure out the flour? Melody, come on up. Sorry, Melody*lynn*. I apologize, Melodylynn. Your mom is right, we should always have our names said the way we want. And again, Melodylynn, my name is *Ms.* Natalie, not Miss—well, that was close. Good try.

Great job measuring, Melody . . . lynn! Now we'll put the sugar in. Who's sweet enough to help me with the sugar? Dylan P., come on up! Oh, Henry, I didn't mean to imply that everyone else isn't sweet too. You're all equally sweet and beloved by . . . wait, where's Jakey? Has anyone seen him? Jakey? JACOB!

Bianca, why are you pointing at the refrigerator? Is . . . is . . . Jacob in the . . . oh, thank God, no. But where is he? Takeysha, why are you giggling? No, please don't pout, it's fine to giggle, giggling is a wonderful sound, but I was just wondering if maybe your giggling had anything to do with Jakey—oh, you were just remembering something funny on *PAW Patrol*. Fine, okay, Takeysha.

So, class, this is no big deal, but has anyone seen Jakey, because . . . uh, I really want him to measure out the sugar for us! That's a good job for Jakey!

Again, Henry, it's not that you aren't also sweet. Morgan? Why are you staring fixedly under the counter—AGH! Jakey! That's where you've been! GOD.

Yeah, you sure did surprise me! I am really fu— very surprised. Okay. Let's get back to the bread. Wait, where's the sugar? It was— Hey, why do so many of you look like you just ate a sugar-dusted donut? Melodylynn? Dylan S.? Dylan P.? Dylan S.-P.? Bianca? HENRY? Did y'all eat that sugar? What's behind your back, Morgan? Y'ALL! Did y'all EAT LIKE A QUARTER OF A BAG OF SUGAR? Ms. Natalie is being very loud because she's WORRIED! DID YOU? Yes, Harper? Uh-huh, I'm going to stop you right there, Harper. This may not be the best time for me to learn the difference between the transept and the quire.

I'm just going to take this bag of sugar and hold it in my lap, and we're all going to play a game I just made up called Look at Your Hands. That's it, that's the whole game. Ready? One-two-three, look at your hands!

I am crying a little bit, Morgan, yes. Just a little bit. I'm a little sad because I just miss Mr. Kenny so much. Okay, if you want to sing "Let It Go," that would be nice, sure. Oh, you'll all sing? Oh, that is actually really nice. I love you guys very much.

So, everyone, when Miss Lara said that the bread machine was a bad idea, I decided to also buy a bag of croissants at the grocery store. They're bread too. Sometimes when we have Cooking Day, it's more about appreciating that we can buy what someone else cooked for us than cooking ourselves. They're on the counter. Gertrude, could you get those for us? That's right. My God, Gertrude, I would be a hot mess without you, you are an amazing four-year-old.

And who would like to get the butter? Dylan S.-P., good job. Let's have a picnic on the floor of the kitchen! Won't that be fun? Now, who wants butter on their croissant? Yes, Harper, I did know that croissants are French. No, I didn't know that the word "croissant" means crescent . . . Let's have snaps for croissants.

Wait. Where's Jakey?

A Letter from Your Child's Teacher, on Winter Holiday Gifts

Dear Parents/Guardians/Interested Adults with Proper Security Clearances:

Hello! First, let me wish you the very happiest winter holiday of your choice! That is, unless you do not celebrate a winter holiday. If that is the case, let me wish you: Hello!

At this time of year, I find it helpful to reiterate our school's policy on students' gifts to teachers, as the faculty was recently reminded to do by our principal, Mr. Gonzales. Referring to the faculty handbook, a publication I have never seen and that my elder colleagues doubt exists, Mr. Gonzales reminded us that teachers are not allowed to receive "expensive" gifts from students in their class. Of course, it is my pleasure as well as my intent to follow the principal's guidelines in this, as in all school directives.

You may immediately wonder what the term "expensive" would encompass. I questioned Mr. Gonzales on just this point at length, and finally received the definition I share with you now. *Expensive* means: "Oh, come on. Gifts should cost less than a Studebaker, okay?" For your information, a Studebaker lacking an engine was recently listed on eBay for $17,500, which I think provides us with an appropriate guideline: please do not give gifts in excess of $17,500 to your child's teachers.

If you require more guidance, I find that it is worthwhile to think of the work done by the person you wish to give a gift to, and the importance of that work to you. Let us consider, say, my car mechanic, Fred. Thinking about all that Fred has done to keep my 2006 Ford Focus running smoothly even as it approaches its fourteenth birthday, I am grateful to him and thus decide to give Fred a gift of approximately $50 this winter holiday season. The same value-to-amount ratio can be used for the conundrum about how much to gift your child's teachers!

Allow me to demonstrate: Were I to have a child, let's call him Toby, I would think over how Toby's second-grade teacher helps him learn the basic principles of reading and writing; teaches Toby the wonders of math, science, and the arts; has occasionally had to evaluate whether Toby's snot is greenish, indicating an infection; once pretended not to hear when Toby informed his father that he could not wait to watch *Law & Order: Special Victims Unit* again; escorted Toby and his classmates to see *Dora the Explorer Live on Ice!* at a stadium in a town an hour's bus ride away in either direction; and has worn the same old North Face jacket at recess every day this fall, even after Toby, perhaps in a fit of joy over the seasonal return of *Law & Order: SVU*, wrote "Dun DUN" on it with a permanent marker. What might the work that Toby's teacher has done be worth, do you think? Remember, keep it under $17,500!

As you know, we are lucky to have three children named Waldo and two named Emerson in our class this year, so I often read aloud the work of Ralph Waldo Emerson at Reading Time. The notorious RWE wrote, "The only gift is a portion of thyself." Wise words, although they did cause Sophia to ask, "Does that mean, like, your finger or something?" and Marcus to answer, "No, like, a portion of your finger." From the mouths of babes! I cannot overlook their point. Perhaps we do overemphasize the personal and handmade during the holiday season. While I treasure all of the handmade gifts I've been given, it's difficult to make good use of all eighty-seven of the handprint mugs I've received in my five years of teaching.

The holiday season is a time of great wonder and beauty, of course, but also a time of intense panic and incapacitating despair. If I can ease either of those for you and your child by taking away the burden of crafting a handmade gift, well, then, may I never shirk my duty. For your sanity and health, step away from the mason jars and glitter. Take your child's feet out of the paint. Stop stenciling with apples. I will gladly accept your store-purchased gift or gift card, so long as it isn't for an amount greater than $17,499.

Yours,

the woman who hears what your child says when she makes two dolls kiss,

Ms. Bennett

Middle School Parent-Teacher Conference Night, in Internet Headlines

DIY: Your Child's Medical Records

When You See What This Mother Asked Her Son's History Teacher to Do with His Understanding of the Louisiana Purchase, You'll Be Shocked!

The Four Best Prepackaged Party Trays Available at the Key Foods across the Street from the School

She Gave an Irate Father a Beat-Up Copy of *The Giver*; When You See What Happened Next, It Will Restore Your Faith in Humanity

Wait Until You Hear What This School Band Does to "Seasons of Love"!

Five Ways to Traverse the School Building without Running into Your Child's Science Teacher

When This Daughter Started Begging Off Gym Because of "Female Issues," She Couldn't Believe That the Male Teacher Dared to Bring It Up . . . to Her Mom!

Must Listen: We Auto-Tune the Guidance Counselor's Preemptive
Speech about College Prep

Are You an Annoying Parent? Take This Quiz about Teachers'
Studied, Neutral Expressions and Find Out!

Here's a Quick Cheat Sheet on the Basic Principles of Geometry So
You Might Possibly Begin to Understand What Mrs. Gold Is Saying
about Jordan's Homework

Señor Smith Does Not Want to Hear Your "Holas," Guys

Thirty-Six New Eye Rolls Your Seventh Grader Will Love!

Eight of the Most Passive-Aggressive Excuses This Woodshop
Teacher's Ever Heard

It's Not Your Imagination: Everyone in the Hallway Did Stop Talking
When You Turned the Corner—Here's How to Handle It

School Security Guards and What They Actually Do All Day:
A History in GIFs

Yes, He's Still the Football Coach, and No, He Doesn't Remember How
You Embarrassed Yourself at Tryouts Twenty-Three Years Ago

Psst!: The Musical Director *Does* Know What the Spring Show Will Be!
She Just Doesn't Want to Hear Your Complaints about
Fiddler on the Roof

This Principal Speaks for All of Us When She Says "Please Call My
Office to Set Up a Time for a Longer Conversation"

Your Child's Complex Social Standing in This Godforsaken
Hierarchy That So Reminds You of *Lord of the Flies*
in Eighteen Diagrams

Quick! Can You Tell the Silhouettes of Your Mom Friends from Those
of Your Mom Frenemies in a Dark Parking Lot?

Here's a Spotify Playlist for the Ride Home That Will Perfectly
Capture the Grim Mood in Your Car: Featuring the Cure, Joy Division,
Johnny Cash's Cover of "Hurt," and Many More!

How I Imagined My Teachers Conversed about Me When I Was Thirteen

The hallway of my middle school, 6 A.M. A light switches on in room 212. My English teacher, Mrs. Elliot, fully dressed and made up, opens her classroom door to start the day. She has been reading Lois Lowry's The Giver *for pleasure and tucks a bookmark neatly into it. She calls down the hallway to room 214.*

Mrs. Elliot: Good morning, Mrs. Henderson!

Mrs. Henderson, my US history teacher, also fully dressed and made up, opens the door to her classroom. She is holding a copy of the Constitution of the United States of America, which she has been reading for pleasure.

Mrs. Henderson: Good morning, Mrs. Elliot! I trust you slept well?
Mrs. Elliot: Indeed! My desk-bed is so comfortable! You?
Mrs. Henderson: Of course! I also enjoyed my shower in the girls' locker room.

Mrs. Elliot: Who wouldn't? Shall we grab some breakfast?

They meet in the hallway and cross to the faculty lounge, which is actually a small diner. They seat themselves and eat the pancakes brought by the waitress as they continue talking.

Mrs. Henderson: I am loath to bring up an unpleasant topic, but did you notice—

Mrs. Elliot: Shannon Reed's face? How could I not?

Mrs. Henderson: That out of the thousands, nay, millions of possible topics I might bring up, the fact that you immediately sensed what I wanted to discuss really says it all. Her face is an international crisis.

Mrs. Elliot: Indeed! It is all anyone here talks about—the students, faculty, visiting parents, kitchen ladies, the secretaries, that nice janitor who is always whistling "Sweet Georgia Brown" . . . Her pimples are on all of our minds both day and night!

Mrs. Henderson: What is up with that? Does she even wash her face? Does she apply Crisco directly to her cheeks?

Mrs. Elliot: I am slightly more sympathetic and once gave her a tissue when she had a nosebleed, so I'd say it's probably just hormones and oily skin—

Mrs. Henderson: —whereas I am the kind of bitch who snapped that she didn't need to tell the class about every historical fort she's ever been to with her family, so I think it's something inherently and unalterably foul about her that has caused her acne.

Mrs. Elliot: It is horrific, truly the worst and most upsetting thing I've seen in my thirty-two . . . ? (*Mrs. Henderson raises an eyebrow.*) Seventy-eight . . . ? (*Mrs. Henderson frowns.*) Fifty-three years! (*Mrs. Henderson nods.*) How can anyone stand to be near her? She's disgusting.

Mrs. Henderson: I know! As the seventh-grade history teacher, you know that I enjoy grading worksheets about Reconstruction every night—

Mrs. Elliot: —sure, in the same way that I like to memorize vocabulary words like "habitual" before bed—

Mrs. Henderson: —of course. But in all honesty, I can barely concentrate because of Shannon Reed's face. Should we say something to her?

Mrs. Elliot: No, no. That's too far. Hmm . . . I know! We should repeatedly let her catch us staring at her while she's taking a quiz or test, so that she feels judged but doesn't know exactly why or what for.

Mrs. Henderson: Splendid! Oh, could we also wait until she passes by us in the hallway and then say something to each other under our breath, something that most likely has nothing to do with her in any way but that she'll think is about the giant pimple on her nose?

Mrs. Elliot: That's mean.

Mrs. Henderson: But, Mrs. Elliot, how else will she learn that she has been judged and found wanting?

Mrs. Elliot: True. Okay, I'm in.

The waitress comes to take their plates.

Waitress: Can I get you two anything else?

Mrs. Henderson: No, thanks. Just send our bill to the principal, Mr. Clydesdale.

Waitress: Will do! See you back here at lunchtime! Oh, and if you see Shannon Reed . . .

Mrs. Elliot: We know—tell her to cut back on the chocolate.

Waitress: Oh, no, I just wanted you to tell her that everyone knows she has a crush on Dirk Rokowsky, she's not fooling us.

Mrs. Henderson: Done!

Mrs. Henderson and Mrs. Elliot cross to two comfortable-looking arm-chairs, each of which has their name embroidered on it. They sit.

Mrs. Elliot: What are you going to do now, Mrs. Henderson? I am going to look through this JCPenney's catalog to see if there are any new Dockers products.

Mrs. Henderson: Oh, that sounds fun. I'm going to write something on Shannon Reed's worksheet and then cross it out, so that she spends the next week wondering what I wrote originally.

A pause. Then both women laugh uproariously as the curtain falls.

Memo to Parents and Legal Guardians Re: Our Updated Schedule for Spirit Days at Mapledale Middle School

Wow! We ladies in the school office—along with Barry, our beloved vice principal for finances, whose desk is in the back left corner, of course—have received a lot of feedback on the Schedule for Spirit Days at Mapledale Middle School sent home last week. We'd like to clarify for the record that, no, we don't think you parents are made of money, and yes, we understand that you only have so many hours in the day. (Also, Barry would like us to mention that he isn't actually involved in the decision-making process around the Spirit Days at all, it's really just the finances of the school district that concern him, but thank you to the several parents who made their feelings about the Spirit Days Schedule clear to him at the Shop 'n Save yesterday.)

So! Let's try again, shall we? In an effort to keep the fun of Spirit Days without forcing any of you to follow through on your various threats, we've updated the Spirit Days Schedule to reflect the suggestions of our students, parents, and faculty. Please read below to see our changes, and as always, Go, Mapledale Sap Tappers!

Week 1

Monday will be T-Shirt Day!

This was formerly College T-shirt Day. We hear you: not everyone is college bound, and college bookstores charge an arm and a leg. So, let's forget all that elitist nonsense and just wear a T-shirt, unless you don't have a T-shirt, in which case we have a stack of "Mapledale 2002 Fun Run & 3K Walk" T-shirts to give out!

Tuesday will be Some Kind of Pride Day!

We had been calling this School Pride Day, but as Principal Nickles asked when we briefly caught sight of him as he scurried into his office last week: "Just how proud are we, given that Mapledale Middle School scored four percent lower than Monroevale Middle School on the statewide standardized tests last year?" He has a point! And he's the principal! So, just wear something that depicts something that you're proud of, or in, or for, or whatever! Show some pride in something!

Wednesday will be Dress Like the Change You'd Like to See in the World Day!

This replaces our annual Maul 'em, Mapledale Sap Tappers! Day. Thank you to our art teacher, Ms. Hallon, for pointing out that such a day could be interpreted as promoting masculine stereotypes and ritualized violence. We agree, and look forward to this more peaceful celebration.

Thursday is Dress as Your Favorite Communist, Why Doncha, Geez, This School, I Swear Day!

Thank you to seventh-grade parent Bill Larson for this suggestion, which he yelled at Ms. Hallon after hearing her suggestion! We're looking forward to seeing lots of Maos, Marxes, and a Trotsky or two in the halls on this day!

Friday is Dress in a Color Day!

Once upon a time, Principal Nickles chose a particular color for this day, and asked everyone to wear it. However, many of you have pointed out that there are unforeseen problems with wearing all white (KKK), all red or blue (various gangs), all black ("promotes Goth-yness," well said, Barry!), all yellow (that cult that makes candles on the outskirts of town), and all pink ("Really? The boys too?" said Mr. Seneca, our beloved and tenured health and gym teacher of the last thirty-seven years). Given all of the issues, Mr. Nickles instead suggested people wear, and we quote, "Whatever they want, I don't care, I have a conference call about the test scores, ladies, please." So, instead, we're just suggesting that everyone wear . . . a color. If you want to!

Week 2

Monday is Sports and Other Equally Worthwhile Hobbies Day!

We hear you: there are way more hobbies than just sports. So wear your jersey or your 4-H apron or your Taylor Swift shirt! Or just carry around your video game console or your multisided dice or your tuba or your copy of *The Feminine Mystique*! Whatever makes you *you*! It takes all kinds! No argument on that!

Tuesday is Throwback Day!

Yes, this one is unchanged. But instead of asking students to dress in the style of the 1950s, '60s, or '70s, we're throwing it all the way back to 2017, the last moment when life, at least for us office ladies and Barry, was not a constant morass of fear, clammy anticipation, and existential unease that the next person entering the office might have yet another issue with Spirit Days, which were Principal Nickles's idea to begin with, anyway.

Wednesday is Very Baggy Clothing Day!
Formerly Pajama Day. Special thanks to beloved and, again, tenured Mr. Seneca for wearing slightly too small long johns for Pajama Day last year, and thus becoming the inspiration for changing this up!

Thursday is Hairstyles of the African Diaspora Day!
This was once Crazy Hair Day. We're already looking forward to eighth grader Justice Monaghan's promised ninety-minute PowerPoint as well as Mr. Seneca's mandatory attendance, the fallout from his comment last year about how every day is crazy hair day for some students. Have we mentioned how hard it is to overturn tenure?! Ha ha!

Friday is Twins Are Distinct People and Should Be Treated as Such Day!
We used to call this Twin Day. Wear whatever you like, but make sure to read the brochures about creating self-identity that Sally and Jake Reynolds, parents of sixth graders Bethany and Anika Reynolds, will be bringing to school that day!

Wow, what a two weeks it's going to be! If you have any further concerns, please do address them with Principal Nickles, who is often at Ralph's Inn on Thursday evenings, and belongs to a competitive bowling league in North Mapledale that practices on Saturday mornings. For further details, see Barry.

　　G! M! S! T!

Part II

High School

How I Came to Teach High School

Although the recurrent pinkeye infections and colds that come with teaching people who don't know how to wipe were wearing on me, the real reason I knew I needed to leave teaching preschool was that I was bored. The first year of working with preschoolers is wonderful. The second year is pretty great, but the poop stuff is getting old. The third year, well . . . I can sum it up best by what I heard a teacher in another classroom tell her class one February morning: "I'm so sorry, but we are not allowed to sing 'Twinkle Twinkle Little Star' anymore. It's illegal." That's exactly it. You just can't do some of it, even one more time, which any parent will immediately understand.

I knew that there were things I would miss. Besides my adorable cuddle-bug students, I was going to (and still do) miss not taking work home with me. I miss daily crafting sessions (and the sort of Zen state I entered when cutting out, say, five hundred paper apples). I also miss singing every day, and reading books with tiny, squirmy kids who get very quiet when they're looking for the monster at the end of the book. I deeply miss the closeness I had with some of my students. When you teach preschool, you help to form the way a child will grow up. That's so special.

Also, real talk? Preschool teachers get the best presents from parents, and I miss them! I like presents!

But I wanted to be able to talk *with* (not just at or for) my students. I wanted some relief from the constant focus teaching preschool requires, as well as the ability to teach slightly differently if I wasn't feeling well, or hadn't slept much the night before, or was nursing a broken heart. And I wanted to talk and read and write and critique words. At that point in my life, in my late twenties, I was beginning to conceive of myself as a writer, a grandiose way of saying that I was starting to figure out that I had more than a passing interest in putting words together, and that I was more than eh at it. I even thought I had the potential to get much better. I figured that spending time helping others learn to write and reading lots of great literature would be good for my writing. (By the way, I was correct.)

———

When I was at NYU, some of my classmates opted to earn certifications to teach elementary grades. My choice to work with teenagers always perplexed them. I tried to explain—those kids were older, they'd get my sense of humor, I could talk to them about stuff beyond our mutual fondness for penguins, I could try to be a good role model—but often I boiled it down to "Look, not that many people really like teenagers, but I do, so I think I should work with them."

It's true: I enjoy teenagers. I like that they have to be convinced to like you. I like that they're figuring out who they are; that's a really fun process to help along. I like that so much of the world is new to them, but they're finding their place within it. I like learning about music, fashion, and art through them. Or maybe I just have sympathy and empathy as the product of an awkward adolescence myself. It ain't easy being green, and I was hugely, brightly, vernally green, so I get it.

Thus decided, I needed only to figure out where to start looking for a high school teaching job. I needed to find a place that wouldn't look askance at the fact that I had little formal secondary teaching experience, except for a short stint in a middle school classroom as a student teacher in Rego Park, Queens. After two years in publishing and nearly the same amount of time teaching preschool in New York, I also needed to find a school that wouldn't be concerned that it had been four years since I got my MA. Tricky, but not impossible, I thought. New York is a big city, and there are a lot of schools there. I just needed one school to give me a chance.

I decided to focus on private high schools, which felt strange because I was the product of a public school education, as was everyone else in my family or group of friends. But I was determined not to teach at a public high school in New York. They were large, violent, and terrifying, all of the city agreed. "Read *Up the Down Staircase*," everyone said. I had. It's hilarious but horrifying, so no, thank you, New York City Department of Education.

As all educators know, there's often a very tight window for getting a teaching job—in New York, it's essentially late May through early August, peaking early-ish as administrators learn who won't be coming back the next year. It's just a frenzy while it's happening, and when it's over, that's it until the next year. You're expected to stay wherever you land.

I applied to *so many jobs*. I can't even remember how many, but it was endless, the cycle of looking for ads, emailing or mailing my materials (this was the early 2000s, the last gasp of purchasing résumé paper at JAM Paper & Envelope on Third Avenue), hoping for a phone call, booking a phone interview, then realizing the job wasn't right for me (or realizing I would love to have that job but not getting it), and moving on.

The biggest problem I faced was a result of the fact that I was unwittingly very lucky in real estate. I had moved into Andrew's rent-controlled apartment in the heart of safe, wealthy Park Slope, Brooklyn, and after he moved out to live with his now husband, Corey, I had kept the place on my own. I know it seems insane to choose a job based on one's apartment, but that place was worth it, the real reason I was able to stay in Brooklyn for so many years on a teacher's salary. It had seven rooms! It was next to a bus stop and over a twenty-four-hour bodega! It cost less than $1,000 a month! I wasn't going to leave that apartment, and any job needed to be within a reasonable commute.

The jobs I was considered for were always far away—I interviewed at schools in deep Brooklyn and the Bronx, but had no way to get to them that didn't require commuting for over an hour each way, including very long walks. I didn't have a car because I couldn't afford one, so driving wasn't an option. And I had no special appeal to religious or similarly themed private schools, except for a Lutheran school in Maspeth, Queens, that offered me less than $25,000 a year to take two buses each way to get to them.

It's been years, but writing this all now still makes me feel how tense I was. I think that if any of those schools had offered me a job, I might have taken it, to be honest, so long as the pay was good. (Sorry, Lutheran school, but that pay: yikes!) But that wasn't happening either. It was a terrific mess, and I was getting very panicky.

And then one early September day, a principal from a school with a name I couldn't quite make out called to ask if I would come out to a place I'd never heard of and interview for a six-week substitute position. I didn't remember sending her my information, but she said someone, somewhere, had given it to her, and they really needed a sub, so was I available to interview tomorrow?

Reader, I was.

The Unspoken Rules of the Teachers' Lounge

1. Obviously, students should not enter the teachers' lounge. To that end, do not send your students to the teachers' lounge for any reason, including fire, flood, or a pressing need for a feminine hygiene product.

2. If you ignore the above rule and send a student to ask Mrs. O'Malley if you can borrow her tape dispenser, know that no adult in the room, including Mrs. O'Malley, is responsible for any horrifying sight your student might glimpse in the teachers' lounge.

3. This includes the way Mr. Nelson eats a ham sandwich.

4. If another teacher enters the room visibly weeping but makes herself a cup of coffee without making eye contact with anyone else, all other teachers are obliged to pretend said teacher is not crying.

5. However, if the same teacher pours herself a cup of coffee, then places it on the counter and leans over the sink sobbing, all teachers present are obligated to send at least one representative to hug that teacher around the shoulders and say, "Oh, honey."

6. Every teacher has an assigned seat in the teachers' lounge. If you're new and you don't know which seat to choose, be aware that it will be the one across from Mr. Nelson.

7. If there is a cake in the school, the remains will be sent to the teachers' lounge. Teachers who take a slice and dislike the taste will agree to quietly toss it in the garbage can in their classrooms without making a fuss about it.

8. If an administrative figure enters the teachers' lounge, everyone should visibly tense but continue about their business as though everything is supercool, no problemo.

9. No couch made after 1998 should be placed in the teachers' lounge.

10. It is a grave offense, possibly punishable by death but definitely by ostracization, to drink another teacher's Diet Coke from the lounge fridge. Diet Cokes do not need to be labeled. Everyone knows whose is whose.

11. If you are invited by a teacher who keeps a secret refrigerator in her classroom to use it for your own lunch or beverage, you are implicitly agreeing not to inform the rest of the teachers' lounge of its existence. Similar restrictions apply to private chocolate candy stashes and undisclosed lint rollers.

12. No one in the lounge cares that your student's mother told you that your class was her favorite.

13. Everyone in the lounge cares that your student's mother told you that you're a terrible person and a bad teacher.

14. Never throw away any piece of paper left out on a table in the lounge, including Avon catalogs from the late '90s.

15. If you receive a teacher- or education-related joke, cartoon, or meme via email, you are morally obliged to print it out and tape it to one of the cupboards in the lounge. If the joke involves puns, your obligation is doubled. These may never be removed.

16. Teachers may flee the lounge without explanation or excuse when the following occur: The principal is rumored to be planning to "swing by" with her visiting son who's at Hofstra; a former student whose name cannot be recalled pops in; Mrs. O'Malley has a new stack of photos of her grandchildren to share; Mr. Nelson brought in tuna instead of ham today.

An Alphabet for the School at the End of Beach 112th

There's a magical place in New York. When I'm there, it's hard to remember that I'm still within the city limits. The weather is often different there than it is anywhere else in the city. There are rarely any taxis. There are a couple of subway stops, but they're run with the kind of dreamy inefficiency better suited to a sleepy Italian village than the NYC MTA. The people there sound like they're from Brooklyn or Queens (or both) but dress like they're going surfing, because they often are—the beach is never more than five minutes away. This Brigadoon-ish place is a spit of land that launches itself off Queens into the Atlantic Ocean, where it curves around Brooklyn. If you've ever flown out of JFK, you've probably seen it from the air. It's beach and boardwalk, skyscrapers and marinas, the cold swell of the November ocean, and the bright heat of a July day. Although it's made up of many different neighborhoods, everyone just calls it Rockaway.

It's better known than it once was, thanks to the national coverage of the devastation Hurricane Sandy wrought there, as well as the subsequent rebuilding and rebirth of its shoreline. But until

2012, if you had heard of Rockaway and you weren't from there, you were a Ramones fan, or you remembered that a jet crashed there almost exactly two months after 9/11, or you were a New Yorker who liked going to the beach. When I first went there, in 2004, I had only vaguely heard of it, even though I'd lived in Brooklyn for about four years by then. If pressed, I would have guessed that Rockaway was in Connecticut, because everything New York–adjacent whose location I didn't really know turned out to be in Connecticut.

There was a Catholic girls high school in Rockaway Park on Beach 112th Street—in that name is everything that makes Rockaway special—that needed a substitute English teacher, so the principal, Geri, called me in for an interview. Even though I wasn't keen on teaching in a Catholic school, and especially not a single-sex one (especially one in Connecticut), I desperately needed a job, and it was the Friday before Labor Day weekend, which meant classes were starting in five days, so I was almost out of time . . . so off I went to that enchanted place.

I'm overselling Rockaway, I know. It's just as dirty, oily, and smelly as any other part of the city, and while it *is* beautiful in places, the trash still piles up next to rickety old buildings, the smell of pee is somehow pervasive, and strangers yell at you for no reason. It is New York, after all. But for me, Rockaway is magical because I got that job, and it changed my life.

Stella Maris High School was the school on Beach 112th. The name means Mary, Star of the Sea, perfect for a school so close to the Atlantic Ocean that the faculty parking lot bumped up against a sand dune. The building dated from the 1960s. If you google it, you'll see that it's a classic boxy design from that time, as school-ish as can be. Stella, as everyone called it, as if she was a friend, had long served the Catholic daughters of Rockaway Park, Far Rockaway, Belle Harbor, Roxbury, and Breezy Point, all the communities on that spit of land. Its reputation was of a good, safe, tight-knit school at a relatively low price, the tuition at least half of what private schools in Manhattan cost. At its high point, longtime faculty told me, Stella had been so crowded that they had to convert the teachers' lounge into a classroom, had to ask some of the nuns from the attached convent to teach.

By the time I got there, those days were long gone. The school was on its last legs, the cost too much for the Sisters of St. Joseph to bear any longer, or so they said. Like much of the Roman Catholic Church in America, the Diocese of Brooklyn was in crisis, combining and closing churches and schools. Fewer parents wanted their children to attend a Catholic school, and there were fewer nuns and priests to teach for free—in fact, while I was there, no priests taught at the school at all and only a half dozen nuns did, all of them over the age of fifty. Every year that I was there, the diocese and the Sisters warned that the school's enrollment had to soar, even though it wasn't really that bad: four full classes of freshmen every year. But all things mortal must pass eventually: Stella Maris closed in 2010, two years after I left.

I miss Stella. It was the best school I taught at before I came to Pitt. There are so many things I want to remember, I can write her an alphabet.

A Is for the A Train

I took the A train to get to Stella. Perhaps the best way to illustrate my gratitude for having that job is to tell you about my commute, which was so nuts, it had to have been an act of devotion. I had to leave my apartment before six, almost always in the dark or at dawn, and walk about ten minutes to the Seventh Avenue F train stop. I'd take the F to Jay Street, in downtown Brooklyn, and switch to the A train, making sure that I got the one heading to Broad Channel, which sometimes meant watching three trains go by before mine arrived.

Once at Broad Channel, an island in Jamaica Bay, I'd get out and wait on the platform for the S train. Often, students from Stella who commuted in from other parts of Queens or Brooklyn would be there, and we'd grimly greet each other, each of us unhappy with our lot in life, whether we were too hot or too cold. What was maddening about that particular moment in the commute was that the S train we needed to ride was inevitably already at the station, just off the main train tracks in a holding area, waiting. But the S shared a track with the A, and the A trains on their way into Manhattan got priority because, after all, who would be commuting to Rockaway at 7 A.M.? Sometimes we'd watch three or four As come through, while the S waited and waited until finally, *finally*, it would lumber out of its holding pen and pick us up.

From the Broad Channel stop the S train ran on a narrow subway-only bridge crossing over the rest of Jamaica Bay and then along an elevated track into and through Rockaway. That early part of the trip was both mysterious and beautiful at any time of the year, in the fogs of fall, the icy depths of winter, or the sharp, hard sunshine of spring and summer. Because the bridge wasn't visible from inside the train, the view as we surged along made me feel as if we were flying somehow, just skimming over the water. The juxtaposition of being on a subway—the most urban mode of transportation—and yet seeming to glide through an almost uninhabited world of water and fog and seabirds stunned me every time. Even on the day I went to interview at Stella, running very late, I was struck by its strange beauty.

The subway let us out at Beach 116th Street, so the last leg of the trip was a brisk walk/near run of four blocks to get to Stella on time. Occasionally I arrived early enough to walk on the beach, or at least the boardwalk, before school, another beautiful aspect of that commute, which had me singing happy Springsteen songs in the sunshine and grimly sad ones in the fog and cold. But let's be honest: I was only there early enough to do this maybe once a month.

It was my great luck that the commute was so beautiful because it was incredibly fricking long. If—*if*—everything ran smoothly, I could go door to door in about ninety minutes. But things rarely ran smoothly because of that S train mishegas. So I was perpetually nearly late, and fairly often actually late. To their immense credit, no administrator ever seemed to care as much about this as I did, but oh, it bugged me. I never wanted to seem ungrateful.

B Is for the Beach

Sometimes during lunch, I would walk out of the front doors of the school, up the sidewalk on the half block to the boardwalk, and then down the stairs onto the beach. When I looked out across the Atlantic Ocean, I would remember that when I'd visited the west coast of Ireland, someone had told me, as we looked across the ocean, "Here, we say the next diocese is Brooklyn."

C Is for Colleagues

Stella was the first school where I had colleagues who weren't all in their first few years of teaching. They were fantastic women—and two token, also fantastic, men—full of wisdom, and eager to share it. I stood out for many reasons, being not Catholic, not from New York, and new to teaching high school, and thus a great recipient for their collective knowledge about teaching. From them, I learned how to make a multiple-choice test, oversee detention, and determine whether anyone was reading the assigned book.

I was also without a vehicle of my own, nearly unheard of that far east in the city. Before our first parent-teacher night, I innocently asked someone in the teachers' lounge about the likelihood of getting a car service to take me back to Park Slope at 9 P.M., and a hue and cry was raised about my vulnerability to murder on the streets of what had to be one of the safest neighborhoods in the city. The other teachers immediately made sure I would never have to miss an event or, God forbid, walk around at night because of needing a ride again. Liz, the talented art teacher, chauffeured me around for four years, and was a delight about it throughout. It still boggles my mind that she would do that without any reward, but at least now her kindness is recorded in this book.

D Is for Diversity

One aspect of Stella that I immediately loved was the diversity of the student body. Even though most of the girls were Catholic, not all were—we had students who were Lutheran (I know this because I once offhandedly mentioned I was Lutheran to a class, and for years afterward, the other Lutheran and Protestant girls I didn't even know would find me to make contact, which always made me feel like a minor character in a British costume drama), Muslim, Jewish, Hindu, and, of course, no religion at all. We had tons of Mary Katherines and Marias, as Rockaway remained strongly Irish, Italian, and Irish-Italian, but we also had girls with Puerto Rican, African American, Caribbean, African, Indian, Scandinavian, eastern European, Colombian, Mexican, Venezuelan, Spanish, British, Guyanese, and Moroccan roots. Many students claimed mixed ethnic backgrounds too, with names like Modesty Hannah Hernandez and Veronica O'Reilly-Castro.

Queens is often described as the most diverse borough in the most diverse city in the world. I have no way of knowing if that's true, but Stella definitely made it seem that way. After years of teaching mostly white students, I was so happy to work in a school that reflected the broad swath of humanity I saw in New York.

E Is for Evaluations

Teachers at Stella sent home midterm evaluations every marking period. The other teachers usually sent one home only if a student was failing or causing mayhem, but I chose to fill one out for every student, which meant that I wrote about a hundred evaluations four times a year. I did it because, especially during my first year, I felt that, like the baroness in *The Sound of Music*, I was there on approval. I had to prove that I was worth hiring back.

One day, as I was filling out the stack of evals in the faculty lounge, one of the other teachers noticed.

"You're filling one of those out for every student?" I nodded. She snorted. "Yeah, okay, we'll see how long that lasts. You'll get over that quickly."

She was teasing, probably out of a little insecurity, and I couldn't really fault her for dragging me for being a new teacher: I *was* a new teacher, and I was definitely trying too hard. I mean, I felt like that was the only appropriate approach to my job.

On the other hand, writing those evals took so little time, and the girls and their parents appreciated it so much. Many parents told me that they had never received any positive communication from a teacher before. A few even told me that they'd stuck it up on the fridge at home. I quickly saw that going the extra mile (if it even was a mile? It was, like, the extra hundred yards! It took thirty seconds per eval!) was beneficial for my students, and went a long way to making our time together pleasant.

F Is for Food

When I taught sophomore English, the students were required to give a presentation of some kind. Not that Stella had a rigid curriculum—thankfully, we teachers were mostly left to teach as we felt best—but there were some general guidelines. Since many of the students were terrified about speaking in front of the class, I decided to assign a "How to . . ." presentation, in which they could teach us something that they knew how to do. I figured they'd be too busy doing the task they had chosen to remember how nervous they were once they got started, which mostly proved true. As it turned out, the presentations were absolutely fascinating, so I repeated this assignment every year. We learned how to wear a sari, apply false eyelashes, test the oil in a car, and, from one sheepish but much appreciated student, how to hide the smell of cigarettes on your breath (after that, I started screening topics).

Mostly, though, we learned about special foods and how to prepare them, since that's what got the biggest response: Italian zeppola, Jamaican patties, Irish fudge. (Okay, I don't know what was specifically Irish about it, but my student said her Irish grand-mother had taught her, and it was delicious, so . . . sure!) Agua fresca, Green Goddess dip, Scottish shortbread. Whoopie pies. Horchata. Lingonberry jam. It was all delicious, and none of us ate lunch that week.

G Is for Geri

Geri was the principal at Stella Maris, and the only good principal I had in my teaching career. Along with the equally adept assistant principals at Stella, Ann and Sister Barbara, Geri was absolutely firm in how she ran the school, making sure every decision was for the girls' benefit.

I have a vivid memory of Geri lecturing the girls about a bodega on the boulevard not far from the school that was reliably linked to drug dealing. She said to them, "Girls, you know that I rarely give you an order . . ." and went on to *forbid* them from going to the bodega, her voice almost cracking with emotion. Hearing that, I realized she was right: she rarely laid down the law so firmly and with such passion, and it had an immediate impact on the students when she did. They got that it was serious.

I definitely filed that away for the future: I try hard to be easy-going about most things except those that really count, which is why my students aren't bedeviled by my complicated heading requirements or page layouts but know that if I catch plagiarism it is the end of all that is good about our class. This moment confirmed another thing I had suspected about teaching: a teacher gets to cry/demand/yell/lose her mind exactly once per class. So make it count.

H Is for Homeroom

The key to why Stella worked—and also drove us all crazy sometimes—was the school's insistence that we were some kind of family, a polyglot hodgepodge of plaid skirts and sensible shoes, door knocker earrings and broad accents, swimsuits under polos and compression socks under dress pants. And the administration's key to instilling that sense of family was that each girl was placed in a homeroom for their entire four years at Stella.

Toni, the teacher I was subbing for, had just had a homeroom graduate the year before, so she was due to get a new freshman homeroom. It turned out that she wasn't able to return that year—although, thankfully, she was back the next, turning out to be as wonderful a colleague as she was a teacher—so I became a real teacher with a yearlong contract, and that homeroom became mine. I'd stick with them, room 312, for their entire high school career. When I told them that October morning that I was staying, there was actual applause and whooping (really, at least one whoop!). It was nice to be wanted. It was even nicer that I wanted to be there.

Like all families, my homeroom was not perfect. We made each other nuts sometimes. I watched them fight, sleep, bicker, complain, and needle. Some of the girls got bullied (though never on my watch, if I could help it) and some were bullies. A few of the girls never felt like they fit in; I thought they did, but that doesn't change what they felt. I didn't always contribute as much as I could have. They watched me figure out how to be a teacher with what I'm sure were rapid changes in style and manner—one day trying to be overly controlling, the next intimating that I'm not like the other teachers, I'm a cool teacher. But all that forced time together, twenty minutes at the beginning and ten minutes at the end of every day, and always sitting together everywhere we went, did bond us.

One story about my homeroom. As I wrote above, my commute sometimes made me late. One day, I ran into 312 with just a few minutes left before first period began, in a frenzy about needing to take attendance. One of the girls stopped me, saying, "We did it already." And they had. In fact, they'd do it every time I was late. A group of fourteen-year-old girls took attendance of themselves and then walked it to the office, my initials forged at the bottom of the slip. And they did it accurately too, never giving an absent friend a break by saying she was in school. I wouldn't have gotten in trouble for turning in attendance a little late, but wow, that still impresses me so much, the lengths they went to in order to protect me. Thanks, girls.

I Is for Interview

As you know, I arrived late for my initial interview at Stella. Geri was remarkably forgiving, and we talked for a while about the job. One of the four English teachers had had emergency surgery, and they needed someone to cover her classes—mostly freshman English, with a middle school class thrown in there, if I remember correctly— for about six weeks. The job, Geri made clear, would likely not extend past that point. She was also clear that she was in a bind. I was too, so that worked out.

Geri took a real risk in hiring me, one that other principals simply wouldn't take. So many times up to then I had made a strong case for myself as a good hire in an interview, and the principal had almost hired me, but then he lost his nerve and hired someone with more experience. Geri took a chance, and I hope I made her glad about it. That willingness to follow one's gut can't be taught, and many people wouldn't be as brave or as honest.

J Is for Journalism

Because no teacher ever just teaches, I was the advisor for the student newspaper and the student literary journal at Stella. I wouldn't say it was hard work, exactly, but it was time-consuming, helping the girls plan what they wanted to write, editing their work, designing the pages, then arranging for the printing. The newspaper was sent to the printer via a dial-up modem and printed on real newsprint, then shipped to us. Very old-school. I loved it when the loudspeaker would crackle to life and Sister Barbara would call me to the main office: "Ms. Reed, your newspapers are *heah*."

I'd faithfully distribute enough copies for every homeroom, and later that day I'd see the newspaper scattered all over the floors of the school, as if we expected to have a horde of hamsters visit. It was always a little deflating, more for the student writers than for me, but it was a good lesson for all of us that few people care as much about a piece of writing as its writer does. Soon, Sister Kathleen, the caretaker of the school who was aces at her job, would have her team of janitors at work, and the school was back to perfect the next day.

(An aside about Sister Kathleen: Once, I was in downtown Rockaway ordering flowers for one of the school's events. The owner of the flower shop was very nice to me, no doubt because Stella Maris ordered flowers constantly—we must have been the reason entire carnation farms stayed in business. But there was a dude in the shop who, once he found out where I was from, started complaining about Sister Kathleen. Apparently, he had once worked at the school as a janitor and "She was on our case all the time about keeping that school building clean! It was impossible! It's way too big!" I turned to him and said, cold as ice, "It sounds like you weren't up to her very exacting specifications," and turned my back on him. You come for Sister Kathleen, you come for me.)

K Is for Kathy

It took me a while to ease into feeling comfortable at Stella Maris. I found interacting with students outside the classroom especially tricky. Most of the teachers at Stella had a mom-ish vibe going on, but I was only ten years older than the students. Everything from chatting after school to chatting on the subway was weird for me. If I saw the girls hanging out after school on my walk to the subway, I defaulted to New York Blankness (a performative stance that says, "I don't see you even though you are naked and screaming").

Thank God, then, for Kathy, a freshman. Kathy is a naturally gregarious person, and, as a native New Yorker, she wasn't the least bit intimidated by my amateur's New York Blankness. She would walk right up and start chatting with me on the street. At first, I tried to answer quickly and let her be on her way, figuring that she was just being nice. Eventually—and this took an embarrassingly long time—I realized that Kathy genuinely liked me and wanted to be friends, which we became and are to this day, as I am with many of the Stella girls who joined us to chat, complain about the S train, or buy Slush Puppies at the deli on the corner.

I know that some would say that Kathy and the other girls were suck-ups, but honestly, they really weren't. Kids like that never are because they don't need to be. They already have As, and are friendly because they're at ease and like their teachers. Besides, you won't meet many teachers who aren't aware when we're being brownnosed. Often there's not much we can do about it, so we politely ignore it, but oh, do we *know*.

L Is for Literature

Perhaps the most startling thing that happened to me at Stella that first year was that I realized, despite my confidence in pursuing the job, I was not actually all that well equipped to teach English. I mean, I was great on vocabulary and pretty good on writing, although I quickly learned that being good at something yourself and being able to teach it to others are two entirely different things. I was shakier on grammar, but we had a very helpful and thorough grammar textbook to which I could refer. I had the girls write in journals at the beginning of every class, so I felt that they were developing their self-expression too. The big problem was literature. I just hadn't read enough of it.

At my first English faculty meeting of the year at Stella, Helen, our wonderfully competent and kind English chair, distributed a list of all of the book sets we had available for class reading, and asked us to decide what we would teach. It was shocking and embarrassing to go down the list and see that I hadn't read most of them. *Jane Eyre*, *The Great Gatsby*, *The Diary of a Young Girl*... these were books that were classics while I was in school, so how had they never been assigned? (And why, on the other hand, had I army-crawled my way through *Tess of the D'Urbervilles*?)

So began my self-education. I took on the typical freshman English curriculum as suggested, which included all three of those books, and started reading. Luckily, I had hours of commute to fill, and I was soon a person who had read most of the books available in the book closet, including *The Crucible* (for where there are fifteen-year-old Americans, there is *The Crucible*) and *Romeo and Juliet*.

The best part of reading those works, of course, was the discovery that a book that was hundreds of years old could still speak to my students (and me) today. We were horrified by Jane Eyre's abusive household, and delighted when she found someone to love her. We were baffled by the passion Romeo and Juliet felt, and wanted them desperately to slow down. We were charmed and appalled by

Daisy and Tom, then devastated by the way they walked away from the pain they caused.

Reading with the girls was So. Much. Fun.

M Is for Maura Clarke

There was a small middle school program at Stella Maris named after Maura Clarke, a Catholic martyr who had attended Stella for high school before becoming a nun who served the poor in Latin America. She was murdered in El Salvador in 1980.

I taught two classes of middle school English in my years there, and they were both hell. Unlike the high school program, the middle school was coed, and the boys ricocheted with aggressive hormones—how could they not, with all of those girls around them? I couldn't get them to sit still, let alone read. That was the first time I grasped that I wasn't the kind of teacher who could get *anybody* engaged with literature. I was not the Pied Piper for "The Gift of the Magi." Individually, every single one of those students was a gem of a person, but oh, collectively, gaaaah.

The funny thing is, teaching those middle school classes helped me to reflect on the benefits of single-sex education: the girls at Stella tended to be more outspoken, more independent, and more invested in their interests (including their studies and future career goals) than students I had seen in coed programs, including myself. As girls in the Maura Clarke program often went on to attend Stella, it was apparent to me that they became *more* self-confident as they became older teenagers, exactly opposite the norm in most coed schools. I had been very skeptical, especially since I was and am a woman who has many male friends (and, to be fair, girls at Stella often complained about missing boys in their school lives).

But the contrast between Stella girls and Maura Clarke students was so strong, I began to see that good could come from separating the sexes in education.

N Is for Never Smile Before December

I was repeatedly told this teaching maxim when starting out as a high school teacher. The idea is that you have to be super tough on your class—lots of rules and regulations, demanding protocols, all with a stern visage—so that they take you seriously. And then you can start smiling at them in December, shortly after they've decided that they hate you.

I sort of thought this was BS, but also, as I've mentioned, I had no real idea what I was doing, so I decided I would be firm and not jokesy like I usually am. My first day of class, I got the schedule wrong, was shocked when a bunch of girls showed up to be taught (I thought they were arriving the next period), and broke into semi-hysterical laughter about how tricky the schedule was. Pulling myself together, I then passed around note cards and asked them to tell me about themselves, including any questions they had for me. I read aloud and answered their questions at the end of class. One was "Are you a nice teacher or a mean one?"

"I'm a nice teacher!" I said. I smiled. Then I remembered my decision and tried to hide the smile. "I mean, I'm firm about things because I want you to learn. And I'll definitely go hard-core, just straight up education if you goof off." I was scowling now. The class looked back at me, uneasy. I couldn't help it: I smiled again, and said, "But I'd rather have fun while we learn. Okay?"

They all agreed that this was okay, and we all let out a huge sigh of relief. And that is how I have always taught my classes. I smile a lot! Smiling is nice! People like people who smile!

O Is for Ohhh MY GAWWWD

This is probably a good moment to mention that about 75 percent of the people at Stella had anywhere from a mild to an extremely strong Queens or Brooklyn accent. Think Janice from *Friends*. As a hearing-impaired person, I've always been fond of just how fricking loud Brooklynites are, and Whoa Nelly, Queens folks are EVEN LOUDAH. It was great. I barely missed a word.

And they were truly fascinated by my Western Pennsylvania accent. "You sound like a character on the TV!" one girl exclaimed. I was also asked by more than one girl if I was British, as my mild accent was apparently closer to a PBS costume drama than anything they'd ever heard in New York. Our differences actually led to small communication breakdowns—once, Kathy asked to borrow a pencil, and I told her, "Sure, get it out of my desk drawer."

I say it with two syllables: "Dror-er."

She couldn't understand me at all, and we went back and forth: "What?"

"The drawer, Kathy, the drawer!"

Until finally the light bulb clicked on. "Oh, you mean the *draw*."

If I may say so, my imitation of the Stella girls' accent was spot-on, as it should have been since I heard it nonstop, and I often delighted my friends with it, although they did tend to think I was exaggerating for comedic effect.

One Saturday, I was walking with some friends through Times Square after midnight. All of a sudden we heard "MIZZZ REEED! OVAH HERE! MIZZZ REEEEED!" It turned out that some of my students were hanging out with their dates on a nearby stoop. I went over and hugged them, chatted, gave their boyfriends the stink eye, and returned to my friends.

"I can't believe that they called over their *teacher*," one said. "I would never have done that in high school."

"Well, it's a special school," I said.

A pause. Then, "So, you weren't exaggerating that accent at all, huh?"

P Is for Parents

Parents at Stella could be *tough*. I once had a parent excoriate me because I used a phrase ("Don't slack off") she found objectionable on her daughter's otherwise very positive evaluation. (Yes, I did briefly consider ending my Evals for All program after recovering from her diatribe.) Another parent was livid that I had failed her daughter, although her daughter had done absolutely none of the work for the semester. Like, zilch. That complaint went to Geri, who asked to see my grade book, looked at the line of zeros under the girl's name, and tossed the book down in disgust as she dialed the number of the complaining mom.

This was another way the admin at Stella were great: they backed up the teachers. But we didn't need to be backed up too often. Parents of Stella girls mostly believed that we teachers were doing the best that we could by their daughters, and almost always took our side. I have so many vivid memories of parent-teacher conferences, which were attended by all, even parents of seniors, with enthusiasm. I learned to try to heap on as much praise as I could so that when I turned to the small, worrying parts, the parent wasn't primed for complete outrage.

"Rhonda is doing so well, and her last paper was really good!"

"Uh-huh."

"And she has been studying for her vocab—"

"Mizz Reed, if I may, what's her grade?"

"Well, she has a B right now, but—"

"A B?! A B?! RHONDA THERESA VINCENTA MACGREGOR, WHY ARE WE PAYING AN ARM AND A LEG TO SEND YOU TO THIS SCHOOL FOR YOU TO GET A B? YOUR GRANDMOTHER IS GONNA BE DEVASTATED."

They were loud people. Rhonda's grades almost always improved. I loved those parents, who almost never assumed I was at fault.

Q Is for Queer

This was before the word "queer" was commonly used outside academia, but yeah, there was a strong, if small, queer population at Stella. As a theatre person, I knew tons of queer folks, but hadn't really considered in that straight, cisgender way of mine that if queerness was genetic, it was present in every population, including youth. So watching girls at Stella come out, struggling or easy as pie, was a great reminder for me, and I'm glad I learned it. Now I look at every class and remember that someone in it is working on coming out of the closet. I ask myself what I can do that helps, usually without ever finding out who it was.

R Is for the Regents

Stella was also the first time I encountered the New York State Regents, a series of standardized tests on the subjects covered in a secondary education. They are administered three times a year (January, June, and August) to students in New York. In order to graduate from an accredited New York City school at the time I was teaching there, a student had to pass five Regents with a grade of 65 or higher: a science, a math, a history, English, and an additional subject test as decided by the school. Many students take more Regents, but that's the minimum. When I taught sophomore honors English my second year at Stella, my class took the English Regents that year, as did the junior English classes, which meant trying to heave all of them—so many girls!—over the finish line to passing.

It was very hard for teachers as well as students. I mean, the actual work of grading the Regents was overwhelming: two straight days spent in the high school library, reading and evaluating essay after essay. But the emotional fallout was even harder. I recall seeing one of my colleagues weeping in the hallway because not very many of her students had passed the Regents in her subject: all that work, yet little success. And now instead of moving on in the curriculum, perhaps learning something much more interesting, she would have to spend another semester teaching the same material to the same girls, hoping it lodged into their heads better. English usually posted better results—American education teaches reading and writing if nothing else—but we still had plenty of failures. The worst outcome was when an entire class passed . . . except for one girl. That happened twice in my time there.

I rapidly got better at teaching to a test, much as I hated doing it, and soon was pretty good at advising students on how to read quickly and well, then write even more quickly and well, so that they could pass the English Regents. But there were always students who just weren't readers and writers (which is fine, we are vast, we contain multitudes) and they struggled. One student failed three times, and then I tutored her after school for three months to help her get ready, and then she failed again and lost her music scholarship to a college she could not otherwise afford. I doubt that college would have worked out for her, but ugh, the nightmare of the whole thing broke my heart.

I hate standardized tests—they mislead in demonstrating students' skills, invalidate perfectly intelligent young people, and mostly test a body of knowledge that is white, straight, middle- or upper-class, and not representative of the majority of students I've taught. You won't find many teachers who disagree.

S Is for Statues

Every floor at Stella had a giant statue of either Jesus, Mary, or Saint Joseph at one end of the hallway. When I was assigned to be the hall monitor, which meant asking the girls to show me their pass when they left a classroom, my favorite thing to do was to sit just in front of the statue and say, "Jesus and I would like to know why you're out of class."

T Is for Trips

I have never encountered a high school with more special days than Stella Maris. I think we maybe had one week in the entire year where we just went to class, nothing special, for five full days. It was great—not only did I love the extra days off, but it made school really fun. Besides the Regents and the myriad days off that the NYCDOE has in order to accommodate the significant holidays of so many religions, we also got major Catholic holidays off: Andrew was always particularly galled that I got to stay home on Immaculate Conception Day ("It is *not* a holiday!" he would grumble as he left for work, especially peeved that as a Lutheran I didn't even have to go to church). We also had in-school special days, including the Marathon (a fund-raising stroll up and down the Rockaway Boardwalk, definitely not at marathon speeds), Career Day, various class retreats, and special masses. And things happened—it snowed, a water main on the corner broke, a pope died, and the MTA's bus drivers went on strike, which meant that Geri picked me up on Flatbush Avenue in order to get me to work because I had no other way to make it there, bless her. (This was right before Christmas break, and finally they closed the school two days early. I can still vividly picture the way the girls sat up expectantly when the loudspeaker crackled to life just before Sister Barbara began explaining this. The joy that followed!)

But the best special day of all was Culture Day (CaulTAH Day). This was a day in which the faculty set up field trips into "the city" (as Manhattan is inevitably termed in Brooklyn and Queens, which are part of the same city) and the girls could sign up to attend them. The girls loved this day, as you can imagine. We took them by school bus into Manhattan, did something cultural, and then allowed them to return home by public transportation on their own. After a couple of years, I was invited to be the co-chaperone of the Broadway trip, an honor and a delight, even when the show was a revival of *West Side Story*, which seemed to be about fifteen hours long. It was so much fun, and while it felt wrong to release the students into Manhattan after the show—like sending baby Christians out to the lions—I got used to it.

U Is for Unhappiness

Life at Stella was not always cuddles and rainbows. A girl OD'd in class (she recovered). Girls showed up with bruises, which we had to report to the proper authorities. Girls had what were clearly mental breakdowns, screaming, crying, and hitting the wall in the hall. There were fights. There were homophobic and racist slurs. Several girls were cruelly ostracized and eventually left. Parents couldn't or didn't pay tuition, and after everything else was tried, their daughters were called down to the office and sent home, an extraordinarily embarrassing event that the administration tried to avoid at all costs but was occasionally forced into.

The faculty had issues too. There was bigotry from a few teachers, and one or two were so hard-nosed about the dress code that you knew there was something up with that. Someone relapsed. Marriages broke up. People got sick. The beloved school nurse had a heart attack. A teacher died. There were arguments and disagreements that would have seemed petty if each side hadn't held on to their grudge so intensely.

The saddest issue for me was when a student realized she was gay but felt she couldn't be honest about who she really was to her deeply Catholic parents. I watched this wreak havoc, as girls fell in love with each other but kept confused boyfriends around as a front. So many people got hurt. It's heartbreaking when you can't keep your students from hurting themselves and one another, which I saw everywhere I taught, including at Stella.

V Is for Variety

If you want to know about new music, hang out with teenagers. If you want to know about a lot of different kinds of new music, hang out with a large group of Queens teenagers, and soon your iPod (remember iPods?) will have merengue, rap, hip-hop, and angry female singer-songwriters where once only circa-1990s alternative bands and show tunes lived.

I don't miss a great deal about teaching at the high school level, but I do miss being immersed in the cultural world that my students were part of. I didn't like everything (sorry, J.Lo) but I loved a lot of it, including, to my great surprise, Eminem. In later years,

I'd impress other groups of teenagers by knowing all the words to "Lose Yourself," thanks to Stella girls and their endless rehearsal for a school show that included it. Feet, fail me not!

W Is for Writing

After a couple of years at Stella, I settled into a pleasant groove. It wasn't the kind of boredom that drove me out of teaching preschool, but I did sometimes feel a little understimulated. The students were so nice overall, and they genuinely behaved well, and clearly were learning. Even though I enjoyed teaching them, I found I didn't always have a lot to do outside of the classroom at least some of the time. (Later, I would look back to this time with an almost palpable longing.) I liked teaching and thought I was getting better at it, but I missed creating things. I briefly considered trying acting again, but after a heart-to-heart with Andrew about what exactly my talents were, and what I ought to do with my life, I started writing more intensively, finding time to do it almost every day.

And I started writing plays. A lot of them drew from what I was reading with the girls, like *Horatio & Ismene*, my short play about what happened when Hamlet's best friend and Antigone's sister meet up. These plays actually started to get produced, and I began, with great hesitation and a sure sense that I was going to be knocked back on my heels soon, to think of myself as a writer. You see where that led.

I couldn't have done that without the reasonable demands placed on me as a teacher at Stella, and I'm forever grateful. And I worry all the time about teachers who don't have enough time to pursue their other interests, and the people who don't pursue teaching even though they might be good at it because they want a more balanced life than what most schools demand—unfairly and unnecessarily.

X Is for Xtravagant

I know I'm cheating with that spelling. I couldn't figure out how to make X-ray or xylophone work.

I don't want to imply that Stella was at all extravagant, because money was watched tightly and not wasted. This was, after all, a school where I made about $35,000 a year. In New York. But they were extravagantly loving to the girls, especially at graduation and the events around it, which seemed to number in the dozens. As I've mentioned, there were flower arrangements galore, and corsages, and, if I'm remembering correctly, flowers for teachers too. We had a senior luncheon at the most amazing banquet hall in Howard Beach, Queens, which sometimes, but not always, featured a chocolate fountain. Every year in the month leading up to the luncheon, I asked Liz a million times if she thought this would be a chocolate fountain year. My last year, my graduating homeroom made sure they had a chocolate fountain and dedicated it to me; possibly the moment of my teaching career when I've felt most loved.

Faculty was treated well too. We also had lunches at the holidays and at the end of the school year, where we received small bonuses and gifts. At every one of these events, Geri would celebrate us, by telling the girls that they'd always be Stella girls, by telling us we'd done a good job by them. And she'd raise a glass and toast us. Simple gestures, but things that most schools don't do, I think.

I've always had trouble saying goodbye to my students at the end of the school year. The first year that I taught preschool, I broke down when I got home, sobbing over not having them in my life anymore. Now I no longer sob, usually, but I still have trouble accepting that these students, whose company I've spent so many good hours in, who've made me laugh, think, and feel, are just, you know, done with the class. And in college, it happens twice as often. Not great.

So I look to the model from Stella to help me—I try to turn that last time together into a kind of celebration, extravagant in feeling if not cost. I bake something yummy for the class, and I tell them that I loved teaching them and will always be their teacher. We talk about what we learned. And when they leave, after the hugs and promises to stay in touch, I raise my water bottle and tell the empty room that I loved them.

Y Is for Yikes

So one time, one of the religion classes put together a display with every teacher's name on it and an adjective to describe them. For some reason, I heard about this before it was actually completed, and before long I was *very* invested in this because I am *very* into people complimenting me. Once it was up outside the main office, I eagerly looked for the cross with my name on it (wasn't that a Johnny Cash song—"The Cross with My Name on It"?). My colleagues were described as "kind," "warm," and "loving." I was . . . "dependable." I mean . . . I was crushed. For once I didn't burst into tears, but wow. The youngest, coolest teacher in the school, or so I thought, and I was . . . dependable. Like an old mule.

Here's the thing, though. I have thought about that adjective for years, and realized that it's actually a pretty amazing compliment. What the girls appreciated was that I was there when I said I would be, graded the papers when I said I would, took them to the field trips I had promised, and generally just showed up, albeit occasionally at a brisk pace and slightly late because of the A train. For some of these students—in fact, for some of any teacher's students—we are the most dependable people in their lives. That's an extraordinary thing to realize, and one that keeps me grounded. I try very hard to keep my promises to my students, implicit or explicit, noticed or not.

Now I am honored to be seen as dependable. I work hard to keep that a true description.

Z Is for Zenith

Graduation was held at the nearby public high school on a Saturday, since our building lacked a large enough space to gather the graduates and their families. To get to that school, I'd take my academic robe on the subway, hanging it up on the overhead railing to keep it from getting wrinkled. I looked so young back then that people often congratulated me on my graduation, which I always accepted with delight. Every year another degree; yay me!

Liz was kind enough to drive me home afterward. She always reminded me not to leave anything in the dressing room at the school, because the faculty processed out of the auditorium at the end of the ceremony and then just kept right on going, out to our cars and off to an end-of-the-year lunch.

So that's how I left Stella in June of 2008, on my way to teach at a theatre-based public high school in Brooklyn. I'd told Geri I wasn't coming back that spring, and in April I'd told my homeroom that I'd be graduating from Stella with them. I really felt like I was—I'd somehow gotten a do-over on high school, and, unsurprisingly, I'd done a far, far better job the second time around. I'd been more popular, kinder, funnier, and better dressed. Would that we all had such an opportunity, the kind rarely presented outside of high-concept rom-coms.

At graduation, when I walked through that scrum of excited parents and giggling girls, waving and dispensing hugs, and also getting the hell out of there, I didn't know what was ahead: that my next school would be a nightmare much of the time, that Stella itself only had two more years in her, that I'd be leaving New York in just over four years, that the writing I was starting to do was going to turn into a whole thing. But I was smart enough to know that a beautiful, if occasionally exasperating, portion of my educational career was coming to an end, and I was sad.

On the way to lunch, Liz chatted about the summer ahead, but I hardly listened. I watched the bay go by. I pressed my face against the glass to glimpse Beach 112th Street one more time. I rolled down the window and thought I could smell the ocean, yes, but also chalk, and incense, and Italian donuts, and drugstore perfume. Or maybe I didn't smell all of that wafting in from Rockaway at all. Maybe it was just inside me now. Maybe I was and am still a Stella girl.

Student Essay Checklist

✔ Reference to *The Fountainhead*.

✔ Touchingly inept definition of a well-known cultural phenomenon: "Rock 'n' roll is a type of bouncy music that originated in the 1970s . . ."

✔ Misattribution of quotation: "As Abraham Lincoln said, 'Do unto others as you would have them do unto you.'"

✔ Use of the word "Nowadays . . ."

✔ *The Catcher in the Rye* reference, often misremembering the book's conclusion.

✔ "A _____ team is like a family" about any team sport.

✔ Use of the phrase "According to *Merriam-Webster's Collegiate Dictionary* . . ."

✔ Scorn heaped upon peers who make a certain mistake, followed by the writer making the same mistake herself: "Unlike my peers, I don't need to use an acronym every time I want to share my emotional response, LOL."

✔ Writer takes a grim turn within list of rhetorical questions he poses in essay: "What is the main character's desire? Do any of us have any desire? Is there anything worth desiring? Why are we here? Why?"

✔ Commas instead of periods.

✔ Broad declaration about the characteristics of all people: "Everyone loves pizza!" "No one likes Minnesota!"

✔ Tautologies; for example, "As a football player, I learned that the game is the reason we play the game."

✔ Sincere attempt to find a positive despite overwhelming odds: "So in the end, even though we set our house on fire by mistake, and my dog lost that fight with the rattlesnake, and the rest of the town tried to tar and feather us, I learned that people are still really good."

✔ Semicolons subbed in for any punctuation except their actual use.

✔ "Since the dawn of time, man has . . ."

✔ Hint of a more interesting story not being told: "The day I got my college acceptance was the same day my algebra teacher was arrested for soliciting. I'll never forget opening that letter from Duke . . ."

✔ Attempt to butter up the teacher/professor: "As I've learned in the only helpful English class I've taken so far . . ."

✔ Attempt to subtweet the teacher/professor: "While some would say Joan Didion is a wonderful writer, she isn't."

✔ One enormous paragraph.

✔ Assertion that writer was somehow the only member of a rather large demographic in the area where they grew up: "As a child with glasses, I was the laughingstock of Peoria."

✔ Closing paragraph clearly exists to fulfill mandatory page count: "In conclusion, it is indeed true that *The Scarlet Letter*, a book by Nathaniel Hawthorne, is a very, very good book that is worth having considered in an essay, as I have done in this essay here."

A Conclusive Ranking of the Students at Hogwarts by Order of How Much I Would Enjoy Teaching Them

As someone who teaches Millennials and Generation Z, I've realized that they speak a language less known by my Gen X peers: *Harry Potter*–ese. I read the books when they came out, but once I started teaching at the college level, it occurred to me that I should read them again, because my students refer to all things Hogwarts constantly. So I ended up listening to the excellent audiobook recordings of the Harry Potter series and immediately I was better able to relate to my students—as well as reflect on just how entertaining and moving those books are.

But the second time through, I couldn't help thinking like a high school teacher, pondering the strange teacher-student dynamics of the books: like, did the other students think Dumbledore was playing favorites with Harry? How did Professor McGonagall manage to teach Draco without slapping him, like, at all? And who of these students could I stand to teach for seven long years?

1. Hermione

I mean, of course! Hermione is super smart and dedicated to her studies, two qualities that aren't always found together in teenagers. You can see her potential to be a bad girl, but she also seems to be respectful of her teachers, feeling that she can really learn from them. She seems to generally run on time, bless her. I'd love Hermione, although I would be sad that she spends so much time helping out dumb boys. (Of course not all boys are dumb, but the two she helps a lot are.)

2. Ginny Weasley

Book Ginny, of course. Smart, funny, outgoing, come on! I mean, who isn't a sucker for a wry sixteen-year-old girl? I'd adore having her in class. I'd write her recommendation letters and friend her on Facebook the second she was safely graduated. Ginny is the best of the Weasleys by waaay far.

3. Neville Longbottom

Okay, so Neville does appear to be a bit of an idiot. But I bet he writes really great essays, because he has had a *life*. And I would like that he's super loyal. So maybe he'd drive me crazy in his first year, but by the time he graduates—wait, do they even graduate in the books? I guess they just have a giant battle, which is a kind of graduation!—anyway, I bet I'd cry hard when he got his diploma.

4. Hannah Abbott

You likely have no idea who this is—she's the first in Harry's class to get sorted by the hat—and that's why she'd be a student I enjoy teaching. I'm guessing she's competent yet completely undemanding, which reminds me of many of the young women I've taught.

Hannah could probably stand to speak up a bit more, or stop by my office hours once in a while. But she won't. She'll just keep turning in A-level work, showing she's learning, inserting herself problematically into my life in no way at all.

5. Luna Lovegood
Luna is as sweet as can be, is always interested in productive debate, and would probably appreciate a female role model. I'm a sucker for students who are needy but too plucky to whine about it. However, Luna is also a conspiracy theorist, which would make her essays super annoying to read.

6. Seamus Finnigan
I like Irish accents, and he seems fine.

7. Dean Thomas
Dean is not a very sensible young man, but he does act around Ginny (his ex) the same way I acted around the young men who broke my heart at his age, so I'd be a little sympathetic. But I'd also be constantly on the alert for inappropriate behavior toward Ginny, which could get tiring.

8. Katie Bell
She's a Chaser on Harry's Quidditch team. I ranked her lower than expected because I suspect that many of her essays would focus on how a sports team is like a family, a cliché that will kill me if I ever read it again.

9. Harry Potter
Yes, yes, he's the Boy Who Lived and all, but kids who stare out the window or at their shoes or fall asleep or never seem to be entirely

focused in class bug me, even though I know that they're often listening—except in Harry's case, he *isn't* listening, usually. I'd also be greatly annoyed by how often he gets called out of the room by admin. How am I supposed to teach him to write well if he's in Dumbledore's office all the time?

I suppose I'd eventually come around on him.

10. Cho Chang

It's not Cho's fault that the only thing we really learn about her is that she's "very pretty," but that gives me nothing to work with. Maybe she's great! Maybe she constantly nods like she's totally following my lecture in class but later writes on my evaluation that I never explained things clearly.

11. Oliver Wood

Captain of Harry's Quidditch team, which means he's another sports person, so more teams = families essays, and probably a little boysplaining about Quidditch too.

12. Colin Creevey

Harry's superfan. Sometimes students who define themselves chiefly as fans can be great, since they tend to be relatively happy souls, thrilled to have a passion that they can tap into whenever they like. However, fans can also have way too much to say about whatever they love, and so Colin might turn in too many essays about how awesome Harry Potter is.

13–14. Fred & George Weasley

I truly, deeply, wholeheartedly dislike pranksters, but I rank them higher than dead last because they were brave, and one ended up hearing impaired, like me.

15. Lavender Brown

I detest giggling flirts, and you know that she's the kind of kid who got her parents to make complaints about teachers who tried to help her mature.

16. Ron Weasley

Look, Ron is the worst. I suppose it depends what grade I would have him in, but honestly, he's a mess throughout much of the books. He doesn't study, he doesn't do homework, he whines, he complains, he's awful to Hermione . . . and through it all, he takes absolutely no notice of the many brilliant adults around him, trying to make him into a better person.

I don't like Ron.

17–18. Crabbe & Goyle

Mostly because they'd stress me out constantly, since I'd be sure they were doing something bad, but wouldn't know exactly what. Also, they'd whine so hard when I split them up for twenty minutes of group work. Also also, kids who think that they're smarter than the teacher when they're demonstrably stupider than shrubbery are awful to teach.

19. Draco Malfoy

Ranked last not because of his evilness, although that is, of course, very bad, but because he is the worst kind of student—a suck-up who would then sic his parents on you when the sucking up didn't work.

Dear Parents: We're Going with a *Hamilton-*Centered Curriculum This Year!

As you parents and guardians of our students here at Upper Eastville Central High School know, student engagement is our principal (ha! get it?) concern. Students who are not thoroughly entertained at every moment cannot learn, of course, so it was upsetting to discover that up to 90 percent of our students report feeling "occasionally bored" or worse while at UECHS. That statistic came from the focus group held at the end of last year, which also ranked our then current curriculum poorly because students disliked those admittedly outdated concepts (such as "English" or "mathematics"). Student responses included: "I hate this school and I especially hate biology" and "Why can't we learn about stuff we actually need, like balancing a checkbook and werewolf prevention?" Enthusiasm was no higher among our teachers. An anonymous faculty member noted, "If I have to teach these snotty-nosed kids about the Electoral College one more time, I'm going to deliberately overdose on Seconal."

As you can imagine, we in the administration immediately turned our attention to ways to make our curriculum more engaging! Several great ideas were proposed by our faculty, such as "We should make school more like the Hunger Games" from Mr. Handles, and "If we stop inflating grades, I bet everyone will get a hell of a lot more engaged" from Ms. LeCroix. While the feedback is appreciated, I have decided to ignore the collective several hundred years of experience of the faculty and instead rely on something I remember from my time working at the small, private American school in Hong Kong where I taught an elective Latin course for a year: Why not build a curriculum around a topic that as many students as possible would find engaging? How wonderful! At that school, I designed my once-a-week class around the subject of elephants, and it was a big hit!

But what should our topic be? The Dallas Cowboys? *The Great British Baking Show*? Vaping? A quick survey of the school gave us our answer: in the end most students were either in favor of or did not absolutely detest the idea of focusing on the Pulitzer Prize–winning Broadway musical juggernaut that's changed the way we look at American history: *Hamilton*! That's right, UECHS—this year we're going with a *Hamilton*-centered curriculum!

What will this look like? That's a great question, and one posed, albeit with more profanity, by much of our faculty. Basically, the idea is that we'll try to make every single class period, at every level, every day, about or at least relate to Lin-Manuel Miranda's Broadway smash, *Hamilton*. If you're thinking, well, that sounds excessive, try replacing the words "Lin-Manuel Miranda's Broadway smash, *Hamilton*" with "required state-wide standardized testing." Whoa! As the kids say, OMG, that's already our grind, amirite? I am right!

So, what does a *Hamilton*-centered curriculum look like? Great question! Your student's day might begin with learning about the

American Revolution in American history—maybe they'll listen to "Guns and Ships," say, and write a little rap of their own. Next, it's off to American literature, where they'll read Longfellow's "Paul Revere's Ride," compare it to the plot of *Hamilton*, and write another short rap. Science is next, where they'll discuss the trade winds that brought Alexander Hamilton to "the greatest city in the world!" and then probably write another rap. Then it's on to math, where they'll learn about Hamilton's financial wizardry and how to balance a bank account, or something like that, maybe rapping. Lunch is a colonial American–style meal—no knives or forks!—and perhaps a rousing sing-along of "The Room Where It Happens." The afternoon brings gym (fencing, which is probably in *Hamilton*), life sciences (woodworking, which is surely in *Hamilton*, right?) and . . . Peggy! Just kidding! And fine arts, which of course will be built around producing our amateur sequel to *Hamilton* called *Hamiltoo*. Our theatre teacher, Ms. Nadine, is putting the script together as we speak, although she did want me to note that she is contractually obligated to do so, and would really rather we do *The Music Man*.

That's the scoop, parents and guardians! There are no flaws with this plan, and we will not be "sorry we went with it by October first" as Mrs. Black warned us! We're so excited to see if we can get your kids to go "a lot farther" by "working a lot harder" even if they're not "a lot smarter." Work on your rap skillz, because clearly that's going to be a big part of the next year. And polish up those buckles and dust off your tricorn hats! We'll see you in the footlights—no, I mean in class!—for Hamilton's birthday!*

---

* Please note, Alexander Hamilton's real birthday is in January. School starts August 27th.

Somewhat More Free

After four years at Stella, I moved to teach at THSB, a small theatre-arts-themed public high school in South Brooklyn that had only been open for a year. I changed jobs because I was very tired of the long commute to Stella (especially getting up at five thirty—for a theatre person, I spent far too much of my twenties arising before dawn). Also, I was sinking deeper into debt from trying to survive in Brooklyn on my pitiful salary. If Stella's administration could have paid us all more, I know they would have, and I would've stayed . . . but the school was almost at its end and that was not to be. Still, although I was very tired and a little bored, I hated to leave. I felt safe there.

Stella was a unique world I loved for many reasons, but especially because of the diversity of the people that made up the school. My world before I got to Stella was not very multicultural; my high school had, maybe, a half dozen people of color in it. My college had only a slightly higher percentage dotting our otherwise bland Midwest whiteness, but the theatre program had been one of the more diverse places on campus, at least. It had nothing on Stella, though, which was a rainbow, no color dominating, or so I thought. I loved that. I loved learning about others' traditions, cultures, and lives. Despite all of the horror stories I had heard about the New York City

Department of Education, I thought that any New York City school would be the same as Stella in that way, diverse and functional.

Nope, I was wrong. I forgot that Stella welcomed girls from all over Brooklyn, Queens, and Long Island, a wide and deep pool that meant a broad swath of students that few other city schools could match, especially public schools. While private schools educated students from the tri-state area, public schools were more likely to reflect their specific neighborhoods, which were as likely to be monochromatic as they were diverse: Brooklyn's Borough Park was still mostly Orthodox Jewish, Brownsville mostly black and Latino, and Brighton Beach principally Russian. Even in more affluent neighborhoods, like my own Park Slope, the average neighborhood public high school student body was mostly made up of those local students of color who didn't have resources to attend a private school.

I also failed to see that while the student body at Stella was varied, it was at least 70 percent white, and the faculty was almost *entirely* white. Like many well-intentioned white folks, I confused "There are more people of color here than I'm used to!" with "This is a truly diverse group of people that is not mostly white, nor solely supervised by white people." Stella was the former. It was a lot better than my high school, and it should be lauded for putting women in charge from the principalship on down, but it still wasn't truly racially diverse. Young women of color were welcome at Stella, but they had to code-switch into a white-majority world. I didn't even notice.

————

From the moment in the winter of 2008 when I first heard about an opportunity to teach at a theatre-arts school in South Brooklyn, I was interested in the school's mission but wary of THSB's location and demographics. I quickly learned that it was one of several small schools that had opened in a fortress-like building that had once held a public high school large enough to serve over six thousand students, making it one of the largest in the country. A quick dive into its Wikipedia page alerted me to why it had been slated for closure: plummeting graduation rates and a number of violent incidents, including the stabbing death of a student in the building. THSB and its sister schools were supposed to replace that school and serve the neighborhood, which included a large low-income housing project across the street.

Despite this history, I was interested in the theatre part of the school, so I was willing to talk on the phone with the school's founding principal, Mr. Calvin. During what I would later find out was a contractually unapproved pre-interview, Mr. Calvin led me to believe that THSB's students were mostly kids who were very invested in acting. Although I didn't ask, he rushed to assure me that there were *plenty* of white kids at the school, who, he implied, came in from Manhattan because they loved theatre so much.

Neither of these was true. We had exactly one white kid at the school when I arrived, and the vast majority of our students in the years I was there were simply neighborhood kids who were lucky enough to have a smart adult in their lives who figured that they'd be better off at a smaller arts school rather than the other giant public high school at the other end of the neighborhood. But since I didn't know that yet, I thought I was interviewing to teach at a small, quiet, focused high school—essentially another Stella. The school might be *in* South Brooklyn, but it wasn't, from what Mr. Calvin said, really *of* South Brooklyn. It just happened to be located there. That sounded okay, because I knew I definitely—*definitely*—did not want to teach a bunch of South Brooklyn kids. Oh, let me drop the euphemism here—I didn't want to teach a bunch of *black* South Brooklyn kids.

I know this doesn't flatter me at all, and it shouldn't, but allow me to give you a little context. In order to get to Stella during my last two years there, I had finally abandoned the endless A train and begun taking the 2 train from Park Slope to Flatbush Junction, a transportation hub in the Flatbush area of Brooklyn where the subway and several bus lines met. There, I switched to the Q35 bus, which took me to Rockaway more reliably and with much less drama than the tempestuous A train. The trade-off for the saved time and reduced blood pressure was the wait at the Q35 bus stop at the junction. It was on the same block as another bus stop, which was in use at that time of day by teenagers heading deeper into Brooklyn to their high schools. Those teenagers were often completely obnoxious, loudly screaming curses at each other, spraying each other with water/soda/whatever, shoving themselves and others, and indulging in both mock and real fights, behavior that would have gotten them detention had it happened inside the halls of any reasonable high school. It was both unpleasant and dangerous, and I'd have been put off by seeing a bunch of white teenagers acting that way.

But those teenagers weren't white. They were mostly black, and this added to my discomfort as one of the only white people at the stop. I'd love to say that their behavior was entirely the problem, not the skin color, but that would be dishonest. I really wish that I had a better spin on this, but I don't. I was uncomfortable because unruly black teenagers have long been presented as a particular threat to white women in the US, and I was not able to get out from underneath that untrue and tired trope yet.

It's not as if I was steeped in racism. My parents did not raise me to walk around in fear of black people. Thanks to them, I grew up venerating Martin Luther King Jr. and his dream, and my faith life was always inclusive of others. Also thanks to my parents, I had traveled widely in the US and the UK, and seen a lot of lives not like my own. Besides, after ten years in New York, I wasn't easily freaked out.

But still, I was a woman in 2008 Brooklyn: I had been screamed at, verbally harassed, groped (or at least some dude on the R train tried, fondling an apple in my backpack), whistled at, and followed. If that wasn't enough to make me jumpy, the kinder people of the city seemed to be vigilant about my safety too. Andrew, who is slightly shorter and definitely smaller than I am, always made sure to walk me at least to the edge of Park Slope after I visited his new apartment in another neighborhood. He had good reason to be alert, as several of our female friends had been mugged. My other male friends always managed to find a reason to walk me to my front door after a night on the town (e.g., playing *Rock Band* and eating takeout pizza). Cabdrivers on Atlantic Avenue pulled over to offer me a free ride because, they said, I shouldn't be walking by myself "around this neighborhood at night." For my high school graduation, one of my teachers had given me a key chain that sprayed mace. I still carried it, when I remembered, although I was much more worried about spraying myself accidentally while rooting around in my purse than I was about being attacked. So: I didn't walk around afraid, but I always knew where my phone was. I carried my keys in my hand. I told people when I got home. I told myself that I didn't walk around afraid, but of course I did.

And always, *always*, the people I was supposed to be most afraid of were young black men. They were the rapists on television and in the movies. They snatched bags and sliced with knives and wielded guns. They were splashed across newspaper tabloids, which I didn't buy, but still registered in my subconscious. The story of the Central Park Five was still ricocheting around New York back then, and I had no idea, not a one, that there had been no "wilding," as the papers had endlessly screamed, or that the accused young black men were entirely innocent. I was educated enough to know that black people made up the bulk of the prison population, but not smart enough to understand the reasons of class and culture and prejudice that explained why that was. My fear of black people en masse was bred and fed by the culture and media around me in those years, not overpowering my logic and general sense of egalitarianism but knocking up against my understanding that the black people I knew, especially the girls at Stella, were no different from me. I understood intellectually that their fathers and brothers and uncles and cousins and boyfriends were the very black men I was supposed to be scared of, so my fear was clearly ridiculous. But I didn't think much about this dichotomy. I remained nervous at the bus stop.

This uneasiness on my part was absurd. At no point was a giant gang of, like, four uninterested teenagers going to turn on me at seven in the morning with dozens of people around. As with many of my fears, it was all in my head.

Hence my deeper discomfort—I had a genuine sense of unease, but also an uneasiness at feeling uneasy. This discomfort is also called racism, by the way. It turns out that I liked my people of color mixed heartily among a larger portion of white people, as had been the case at Stella. I did not like being the only non-POC around. I did not like those kids.

And I certainly didn't want to teach at those kids' schools. After I got on the (mostly white) Q35 and headed toward Stella, as I settled in my seat, I'd think, God, what if I taught at *their* school? What if every workday was like my ten minutes of anguish at the bus stop every morning? I always felt so grateful for the well-behaved students at Stella, so glad that I got to teach them and not those other, awful, kids. It never occurred to me that not a single person had ever gotten hurt or truly bothered me at our stop. That the Stella girls' friends and cousins went to those schools. That maybe I should examine my feelings a bit further.

So you can imagine my highly reasoned and prejudice-free response after I accepted Mr. Calvin's offer of an in-person interview with the hiring committee at THSB. When mapping my trip to the interview, I realized I would need to take the 2 to Flatbush Junction again but then walk to a different bus stop to take the B6. Guess which stop that was? Yep. My response was, essentially, "Oh, crap."

I went, but with a giant lump in my throat. On the day of the interview, I arrived at the bus stop. Although it was pretty chill then in the late afternoon, I could picture the screaming kids. I reminded myself of Mr. Calvin's assurance—which was finally making sense—that the school was diverse and quiet.

I boarded the B6 and was the only white person on the bus. On that particular ride, no one said or did anything to make me feel singled out. I mean, of course they didn't—why would the people, commuting home after a long day of work, care whether a white girl was on the bus or not? But wow, did I feel out of place. I would not see another white person until I entered the school building and found Mr. Calvin waiting to take me to the interview. I was uncomfortable, and really continued only because I couldn't imagine reporting back to my friends and family that I had abandoned ship because I was scared.

On the ride, seated among mostly silent, mostly tired people who were lost in their own thoughts after the workday, I was still uncomfortable. I felt like I was inserting myself into a community where I did not belong. And I was. I was a racial minority for the first time in my life. I had never felt like that. My life before, although varied and complex, was always in the company of other white people. Here, I was on my own.

Eventually it would turn out that lots of faculty at THSB took the B6, so I usually was not the only white person on the bus, although it would happen again, especially when I stayed late to work at school and rode the mostly empty bus back to the junction. And my fear would come true: I was occasionally harassed by other riders about my race, like the time a drunk guy in front of me in our line to board told me that the bus "isn't for the likes of you." (A woman in front of him told him to shut up and sit down.) But more often than not, I sat with my fellow theatre teacher and friend Danielle (who's white) and talked about what we had each done the night before, or with a student (black or Latino or both) and talked about music and shows. Once I sat with Leroy, a student with a great sense of humor, and we cracked each other up by pretending we were going to join hands and start singing "Kumbaya" together, touching all the people on the bus with a musical show of our ebony-ivory friendship.

In other words, with time, my commute became just that—a boring trip—instead of an opportunity to think about my race constantly. But that was far off in the future, and on that first ride I had to confront the uncomfortable reality that I noticed and cared a lot more about being part of the majority race than I had thought. Now I recognize what a gift this was, to have even an inkling of what it's like to definitively not fit in because of the color of your skin, but I sure wasn't at that enlightened place on my first bus ride.

The weird interview with a diverse group of female faculty members went fine. I accepted the job in April, wary but really in need of that salary. I figured I had four months to not think much about that bus ride, and I proved to be adept at doing just that, because being in the majority race means that you rarely have to think about race at all. That August, I started at THSB with the usual slate of grown-ups-only professional development workshops that can leave you feeling that teaching is both easy and a little dull. Meanwhile, I looked forward to meeting the quiet, diverse group of students I'd been promised. Somehow, I still had not quite grasped that I would be teaching exactly the kind of obnoxious kids I had so disliked at the bus stop. When faculty who had been in THSB's building for years told me to expect mostly black students—"a white face is as rare as an albino

tiger," one said—I still didn't get it. I also missed my new colleagues'
attempts to prepare me. I still pictured Stella's student body. I didn't
understand that Mr. Calvin wanted to believe he was running a quiet,
diverse school, so that's what he said he was doing.

Then we had our first day of classes.

I'm embarrassed to tell you how horrified I was by how those
kids, who would very soon become *our* kids and *my* kids, acted.
How their energy, which I would soon love and now miss, unnerved
me. How I couldn't keep up with their slang, didn't recognize the
music they played constantly, and was completely confused by the
way they greeted each other and, when they were feeling benevo-
lent, me. I didn't understand that these kids felt no need to act like
they did in a white-majority setting, tidying up their manners and
attitude and tone to please white folks. They were, after all, not in a
white-majority setting.

Not only that, there were—horrors!—boys at this school, which,
okay, I take the heat on that one—no one had promised me an all-girls
school, whoops. I was used to Stella's feminine energy, which tended
to run calmer, with less aggression. That was gone. Oh, and have I
mentioned that instead of chaste Catholic school uniforms, everyone
wore whatever they wanted, which included a few outfits so skimpy
(it was still ninety-plus degrees) that I blushed? The noise level was
loud and *constant*. We were Mr. Calvin's promised quiet retreat only if
the comparison was a school that hosted a daily Megadeath concert.

THSB was about 95 percent African and Caribbean American
(with Latino students making up most of the remaining 5 percent),
with a faculty that was white, Asian, Iranian, Latina, African American, and more. While the school's principals were always white,
most of the other administration was black. It was essentially
a monoculture school run by a diverse faculty. It was like I had
switched Stella's attributes precisely. At the end of the first day, I

went home with a headache, teetering on the edge of despair, I was so undone. I contemplated quitting.

Most teachers know this feeling, which runs rampant during the first week of school—it combines "Lord, what have I done?" with "How quickly can I get out of this?" and a dollop of Beckettian "I must go on, I can't go on, I'll go on." My feeling was exacerbated by the reemergence of that discomfort I had never really dealt with back at the bus stop. I sensed that I needed to, pronto.

I managed to keep myself from emailing Mr. Calvin that I wouldn't be back because he hadn't been—ahem!—completely forthcoming with me. I talked to Andrew about how I felt, telling him (and myself) that Stella had an unusually well-behaved student body, which I could not expect anywhere else in New York. Besides, I wanted to rise to the challenge THSB posed for me and overcome my own problematic thinking. I wanted to teach all of the kids at the school, but to especially connect with those smart, nerdy, dramatic, hardworking, quiet kids at THSB, no matter what color their skin was.

Andrew asked me if anything good had happened at school that first day, and I remembered something: I told one class of freshmen something about reading Shakespeare together, and one of the kids had perked up, saying, "Like, Macbeth and his witchy shit? Cool." A student in one of my classes—I had no idea who, exactly—liked *Macbeth*. My people were in there. Not my white people. Much better: my theatre people. My book people. My sardonic aside people.

So I went to school the next day. And the next. And the next. I got used to the noise level. I got used to the boys and the clothes. I started to make some friends, both in the faculty and among the kids, including Dwight, who turned out to be the *Macbeth* kid. And then somehow, I became part of the community. Not the African American community of South Brooklyn (though few people made me feel unwelcome) but of our weird little world at THSB, where the white adults were haplessly in charge and the black kids were often there to learn, at least a little, and where everyone talked about August Wilson and Dwayne Wade quite a lot.

That said, there were differences I learned to spot, and hate. I saw that my skin color provided me with some protections that my students did not enjoy. There was a takeout fried chicken place across from the school where we all grabbed a delicious, if unhealthy, lunch. When I first went in, I was startled to see that bulletproof glass stretched across the counter, supposedly protecting the cooks and cashier behind it, a reminder that the neighborhood was not considered safe. Ahead of me in line, two of my students yelled through the glass's small holes to order. The cashier wasn't openly hostile to them, but he certainly didn't beam at them like he did me. He also didn't apologize to them about the glass, the way he did to me. Maybe he was being flirtatious. Maybe there were good reasons to have bulletproof glass. Maybe I got free onion rings because I had white skin.

I saw the difference again when Danielle and I escorted a class to see a show on Broadway, the first time for almost all of them. It had been a good day so far. It was one girl's first trip to Manhattan, and she swooned with vertigo when she first exited the subway at Forty-Second Street, screeching, "Ms. Reed, the buildings are *too tall*!" which made us all laugh, including her, after she recovered. True, I had noticed that the theatre's director of education was a little nervous when she greeted us, but we had prepped our students well, and they were genuinely interested in the show. They were a little bit more vocal than maybe your average old white folks audience—Dwight, seated next to me, audibly said, "Oh, no, he did *not*" when a twist was revealed—but the actors came up to us afterward to tell us that they *loved* our enthusiasm and excellent questions at the talk-back after the performance.

So all was well, until we got on the train to head back to Brooklyn. Danielle took one group of students with her on the F, while I escorted the other half on the 2. Since I constantly worried about the train leaving without one of my students (no child left behind is the promise, after all), I always had them board first. Because it was rush hour, the train was more packed than our middle-of-the-morning trip had been and thus I got to see what a bunch of white faces looked like when ten excited black teenagers boarded the train. They didn't look happy. They looked—I recognized it right away—not that different from the way I looked at the bus stop back in my Stella days: a mixture of annoyed, aggrieved, scared, and ashamed at being scared. Then I stepped onto the train and started bossing the kids around, telling some to take a seat and others to hold the railing, and in general, doing my job, which happened to make it clear to those passengers on the train that there was a white person in charge. I hated their relieved faces. I should have told them that the kids were revved up from seeing a Paula Vogel revival at Second Stage.

Incidents like these particularly galled me because I was learning more and more to value my students. I'm always, forever, on their side, anyway. But seeing them prejudged like that pushed me even closer to them. It wasn't that I felt sorry for them. I was just so angry that the world was already against them. How could anyone be afraid of Dwight, or Maddie, or Charisma, kids who bantered, and flirted, and thought, and read, and just generally wanted to live their lives as twenty-first-century teenagers in the greatest city in the world?

Besides, I was growing to love their culture. Like many minorities, I wanted to fit into the majority, and unlike many minorities, I still carried quite a bit of power, so my students were eager to teach me—and I like to think they were flattered too. I had learned a great deal about other cultures at Stella too, but it had been more of a buffet than a deep dive—and I already knew quite a bit about Catholicism from growing up in a deeply Catholic part of the country. At THSB I was truly a newbie, so for perhaps the first time in my life I developed what the Buddhists call "beginner's mind," a sense of openness and eagerness to learn. Some of my lessons were pitifully simple: I learned to fist bump. I learned what "aight" means. I learned why Jay-Z is called Hova. I started saying "Word" and "My bad"—self-consciously at first, and then just because they're perfect expressions. I learned new music, new dances, new ways to wear scarves. I learned that Kwanzaa isn't actually that much of a thing. I read all of August Wilson's plays, which somehow had never been assigned to me to read during the two degrees in theatre I had earned. Baby steps, but all of this learning helped me better understand and appreciate my students. They weren't exotic others, they were just people. We were learning to enjoy the give-and-take of living next to one another. I gave them Gene Kelly's performance of "Singin' in the Rain." They gave me Nicki Minaj's verse on "Monster."

And my students, or some of them anyway, were so patient with me. On the day before school pictures, one girl who'd worn a head wrap every day until then showed up with long, flowing hair. Without thinking, I said, "You have new hair!" So, laughing, she taught me what a weave is.

I want to be clear: it's not that my racism cleared up, like a pimple with enough drying cream applied to it. I remain a product of privilege and a racist society. But my stereotypes withered without any sun to feed them. They had never been strongly held to begin with, and taken out and examined, they didn't make any sense.

I compared what I knew of my students to the faces of the cashier at the chicken place, or the people on the train, and saw which side I was on. My students could be difficult, but they had good reasons to be that way. And they were also sharp and smart and beautiful and kind. The violent, thuggish young black man I was supposed to be afraid of was not someone I recognized in most of my students, and since they were the only young black men I knew, it wasn't hard to change my understanding. There were a few students I was afraid of, as we all were, because they were violent and angry. But the really unnerving ones were few and far between.

We didn't talk about race all that often among the faculty at THSB. The problem of racism was apparent and apparently unfixable, at least by twenty very overworked, put-upon teachers, so why waste our precious minutes railing against it when there was so much to do? We were most often too busy complaining about our dreadful administrators, whose choices kept us from helping our students as well as we ought to. When race came up, it was usually because we were grumbling about a student calling us racist for implementing fair and logical rules. Erica, a white theatre teacher who joined the school in its third year and who quickly became close to Danielle and me, once had a student tell her she was "like the KKK" because she asked him why his homework was late. We understood that our students used words like this because there's a lot of power in them, but they still hurt, especially when, like Erica, we were just trying to do our best for them.

Most of the students didn't mess around with name-calling like that. When the other students heard their classmates calling their teachers prejudiced, they rolled their eyes and said, "Some people want to be victims," and went back to whatever they were doing. I remember one girl telling me, "Look, I'm not going to do my homework, but I'm also not going to call you a racist for telling me to do my homework. I should do my damn homework! I'm not gonna, though."

To our credit, I don't think any of us saw ourselves as white saviors, riding in to rescue the poor black kids from the ghetto. I didn't expect to save my students from poverty just by being whitely present, and no one else on the faculty did either, from what I saw. Besides, a great many of us were not even white. Can you be a Pakistani savior? We did have a few starry-eyed Teach For America teachers who arrived with visions of *Dangerous Minds* and similar movies in their heads, sure that they would be *the* person to find the black Rembrandt or Marie Curie in our midst. But they pretty soon figured out that a) the teachers in those films worked a hundred hours a week, which isn't sustainable, and b) many of the students already had people in their lives helping them find their talents and encouraging their dreams. Our job was to teach them what we could and find them opportunities, not to reveal to them startling truths like music is good or science helps people.

Which is not to say that no saving ever took place: one of our faculty members adopted a young woman after she was kicked out of her home, and a bunch of us banded together to secretly support a notably hardworking student who got a full scholarship to college but had no other resources to draw on for books or a warm winter coat. But these were exceptions. From a student who got into one of the best universities in the country to another who's currently touring with a prestigious jazz band, it was usually their families who really supported and helped them, whether a strong single mother or a full array of parents, stepparents, grandparents, and pushy cousins. Those of the faculty who cared just lent those students our support and taught them as best we could under the circumstances, urging them not to give up. Our students almost invariably rose and fell because of their families' support or lack of it, not because of us.

Don't get me wrong—it was nice that my mind was expanding and that I was becoming less racist, but the big picture was still oppressive. The basic setup of society in America was and still is racist. Our school was poor, and it showed: we lacked a decent library, computers, new textbooks, basic supplies, and the ability to attract top-notch teachers because our students were not deemed worthwhile. There should have been a faculty of accomplished black teachers for black students. Better, the neighborhood should not have been so segregated at all. Instead, it had become the center of a Venn diagram of black kids and young white women in New York City. And our students understood the problems quite well. Once, a student joked to me that there must be a law requiring all young white women in America to teach for a year, the way Israelis have to serve in the military.

As interested as I was in learning about Black American culture, I certainly did not qualify as ready to teach it. It only took me one experience to realize that. Mr. Calvin had decided that the faculty should try to teach more cross-curricular units, and suggested American slavery as a topic. I put together what I thought was a very interesting presentation on slavery for my freshmen, only to be met with row after row of stony expressions. They weren't bored, I realized. They were angry.

"What's up?" I asked.

"We've been learning about slavery since sixth grade," Bianca said.

"Yeah, can we learn something else about black people, please?" Dwight agreed.

On my commute home, I thought about this, and realized how awful it would be to be taught the same depressing topic about my people year after year. I mean, what if I was promised lessons on the Irish people, but instead of learning about Yeats or book illumination or the Gaelic language I was presented with the war in Northern Ireland for the fourth time? I couldn't throw out the slavery curriculum entirely, because Mr. Calvin insisted on it, and other teachers were counting on me to cover some of it. But I could find more interesting ways to teach it.

So the next day, I asked the class what questions they still had about slavery. It took some prodding, but eventually they agreed that they did wonder about a few things. From there, I found what information I could, or asked them to research with me. They wanted to know about slave rebellions—"Why did we put up with that slavery shit?"—so we read about Nat Turner. They wanted to know if there were any really smart slaves, so we read some Frederick Douglass and wrote about Harriet Tubman. We explored the wild truth that free black people in the American South owned slaves before the Civil War. And I presented my finest piece of research: many of the avenues and streets in Brooklyn are named after the Dutch settlers who founded the city—settlers, that is, who had owned slaves. Dwight told me he'd never walk down Marcy Avenue again. The next day, he told me he'd been reading up and planned to move to Harlem someday, "where I can walk up Malcolm X Boulevard."

All of that information was entirely new to me too (and it still creeps me out that one of the best public high schools in the city is named after Peter Stuyvesant, the last Dutch governor of New York, who owned forty slaves). That unit was better because instead of assuming I knew everything and that they knew nothing, I asked them what they didn't know, and what they wanted to learn. It flips the idea of teaching on its head to acknowledge that your students know a lot more about something than you do, but it was a great thing to learn and experience—a lesson that has stayed with me, and, I hope, with those (no longer) kids.

I taught Langston Hughes's work to this class too, as a precursor to reading the play *A Raisin in the Sun*, as the playwright Lorraine Hansberry took her title from Hughes's poem "Harlem." We liked "Harlem" well enough, but most of the students liked my favorite of Hughes's poems better. It's called "Theme for English B," and is written in the voice of a young college student who's been told to "Go home and write/a page tonight./And let that page come out of you—/Then, it will be true." Hughes's narrator goes on to write a short biography, and includes a mild manifesto of pleasure: "Well, I like to eat, sleep, drink, and be in love." The ending is addressed to the instructor of the narrator's English class, who gave the assignment: "As I learn from you,/I guess you learn from me—/although you're older—and white—/and somewhat more free." Bernice pointed out something I'd never noticed before, that the teacher is only *somewhat* more free. She suggested that Hughes wrote it that way "Maybe because the instructor's a little racist"? She was right, I realized. Racism obviously hurt my students more than me, but it hurt me and other white people as well, denying us the opportunity to live in harmony with all, not to mention the gifts that could help everyone but that are too trapped in brains that aren't allowed to be free. All of us can be only *somewhat* free in a racist society.

Because our school was so small, we really got to know each other well. This was not always good, of course, but it sometimes meant that natural reticence and distrust eventually wore away, from day after day spent together. If many young white women are taught to be afraid of young black men, well, it makes a lot of sense that young black men are taught to be very wary around white women, if not to stay away from them entirely. Emmett Till's story is well-known, and the warning of his short life is taken seriously. But after a while, many of these young men realized most young white woman teachers were not going to do them any harm, a lesson we had already learned about them.

I'm not sure why I have a special place in my heart for the young men I taught at THSB—of course, they were lovable, but not more so than the young women. Perhaps I was simply aware, even then, that they were coming of age in a country that particularly didn't like them. Perhaps I remembered, guiltily, how they had scared me. But in any case, the friendships I formed with them are some of the highlights of my time at THSB. There was Dwight, the guy who dug *Macbeth* and wanted to walk up Malcolm X Boulevard—he was a gifted rapper, freestyling the plots to many Shakespearean plays to the class's delight. And Dennis, a young man as smooth as he was angry, who wrote all of that intellect and outrage into a splendid play we saw performed on an Off-Broadway stage his junior year. There was Marc, who broke my heart when I helped him write an essay that started off being about football and ended up being about watching his stepfather bleed to death after being shot in a park the summer before. And Jacob, who won a national acting competition on a Broadway stage, dazzling us all with his talent and charisma.

And I can't forget Malik, who gave me a motto when we discussed the principal's deteriorating wardrobe one day. Mr. Amash, our second principal, had started out his first year in well-cut suits and a snappy tie, but after a few months, as he perceptibly lost his enthusiasm for the job, looked much more bedraggled. Malik, like many of the kids a sleek dresser, complained that Mr. Amash had worn an untucked dress shirt over stained cargo pants to work.

"What's next?" he said. "Board shorts and a T-shirt?"

"Well, you know," I responded in the benign voice I used whenever I didn't want to take sides. "To each his own."

Malik shot me a look of disgust. "Yeah," he said. "To each his crazy-ass own."

A life philosophy was born.

There were also the brothers Rey (Peter and Drake, each a delight), and handsome and talented Donatello with the voice of an angel, and the class wit, Leroy, and smart, helpful Antonio, and so many more, all of them complex, interesting people, who were coming of age with verve and a growing awareness of life's potentials and flaws.

If I bonded with the young men of THSB over their performative skills, the young women I usually came to know in more quiet settings. They drifted into my classroom after school to hang out, often before heading off to drama club or musical practice. Since I helped with those performances, I also got to see their talents: One girl, Michelle, had a great singing voice and was trying to decide between becoming an actor and a lawyer. Another, LeeAnn, was an undocumented immigrant who wanted desperately to go to college. She and I spent hours talking about books. Jeanie, one of the few white kids in the school, had a disability, and we talked about what it was like to go through life differently abled. And Bernice and LaQuanda seemed to pop by almost every afternoon to tease each other, talk about theatre, movies and TV, and make me laugh.

A lot of what brought the school community together was unhappy: The shooting death of our student and classmate Stan. Difficult and disliked principals and their foolish policies. Stress over Regents tests, college applications, and next steps. But we did share two of the happiest days of my teaching life on and after Election Day 2008. There was no school, but teachers had an in-service day. I woke up even earlier than usual and walked to my polling place on the next block to vote. Even at 6 A.M., there was a line. Once I was at THSB, the faculty checked in with each other—reporting on how long the line was at our polling places, and sharing whatever news we could find online about how the vote was shaping up. A general sense of approaching joy was everywhere. When I saw my friend Sheila, our stunning school secretary, coming down the hall that day, we each started weeping and hugged each other as if we already knew, even though it was only one o'clock in the afternoon.

But that was nothing compared to talking to my students the next day. We had all stayed up too late to make sure it was real, to hear the acceptance speech of the country's first black president.

And then they had partied in the streets—champagne and fire-
works, all over the city. I knew this was true, as I heard the shouts
and pops from my bed in Park Slope, and fell asleep smiling. So we
were all bleary-eyed the next day, but a sense of contentment was
pervasive. My students talked about feeling hope, that maybe there
wasn't a limit to what they could do if they wanted. I remember
one young woman marveling, "Michelle's skin is *darker* than mine."
Another said his grandfather had cried, the first time he could ever
remember seeing that. To see such an astounding historical event
among the people it meant the most to was profoundly powerful to
me, and I think it meant something to the kids to see their teachers
so affected and proud. It brought us all closer.

One other happy memory is worth sharing, because it's what I
often recall when I think of what I loved about THSB. One day in my
third year of teaching, long enough into my run there that not only
was I not scared but I thought myself a fool for ever having been
scared, one of my students came to school wearing a pin that read
"I'm Black and I'm Beautiful." We all loved it. I no longer remember exactly how this happened, but the pin started getting passed
around—every period, a new student showed up in my class wearing it, and then it traveled around from student to student while
my back was turned (and yes, maybe I found myself with my back
to the class more often than usual that day, ahem). Dark-skinned,
light-skinned, natural hair, weave, boys, girls, they all beamed as
they wore the pin and I said "You *are*" to each of them. Toward the
end of the day, one of our Latina students ended up wearing it. She
grinned too, and we all told her she *was*. Then the Israeli kid got to
wear it. Somehow I ended up wearing the pin, then sort of forgot
about it, until I walked down the hallway after last period saying
goodbye to my students and wrapping up the day. It was a joke, and
I grinned, and people laughed, but there was also something in that

laughter that I could almost name: some sense of pride that I would even want to be black, that so many of us wanted to be.

But by then, after three years among my beautiful and black students (and my beautiful and Latino or white or whatever students), I did feel proud to borrow being black. By then, I knew so much more about the history of Black Americans. I'd read and taught Douglass and Truth and Baldwin and X and Wilson and Hansberry. I knew who Stuyvesant was and what he'd done. And while I'd never know enough of their history and music and culture, I knew our students. I'd watched them struggle against overwhelming odds, and sometimes succeed. We'd graduated our first class, and though I sensed our administration had served them poorly, I also knew that some of them would end up with a college degree and a job that could raise their whole family up, because those kids would work and work and work. Black was no longer aggravating or scary. It didn't scare me. I respected Black. I was proud to borrow it as an identity for a few minutes. I was sorry to have to give up the joke and give that pin back. Black was, and is, beautiful to me.

———

Oh, sorry. One more thing about the commute. I knew I was over any remaining unease one early-winter day when I waited at the B6 bus stop, playing on my phone. As a girl came around the corner, mock-fighting with her friends, she slammed into me. I snapped, "Step off!"

"Sorry, miss!" she screamed as they ran off.

I went back to my phone. It wasn't scary at all. Annoying, but not scary. The fear had always been in my head.

Random School Motto Generator

Pick one from each column.		
Freedom	Begins	Now
Learning	Grows	Everyone
Education	Flies	Higher
Here, We	Believe(s) in	Tomorrow
Honor	Learns	Potatoes
Wisdom	Begets	More Wisdom
We Are	the	Champions
Our Journey	Is to	Wisdom
Footsteps	in the	Wings of Love
Sic	Semper	Tyrannis
Our School	Is a	Place
Building	Our School	as Expected
Quality	Is the Vague Word	We Extol
Multicultural	Abilities	Prized
Vague	Platitudes	Presented
Always	Trying	Reasonably Hard
Children	First	Except on In-Service Days
We Care	about	Kids
Opening Doors	Is the Metaphor	We Went With
School,	Family,	Community
Success:	Nothing Less Accepted	at Least until June

The Other Class

One of the most helpful techniques I've stumbled upon in teaching is to have another class to refer to, a class that is clearly not the class you are, at that moment, teaching. Referring to "last year's class" is somewhat helpful, but it's even better if you're currently teaching this Other, perhaps mythical, Class. You can use the idea of that Other Class almost without limit. Blame things on them. Attribute qualities to them. Make them the butt of your jokes. Esteem them. The legendary Other Class will save you, time and again.

I realized this when I was at Stella, perhaps in my second or third year of teaching high school, when I met my first, real Other Class. What often happened is that I would present my first-period English class with an assignment—let's say an essay on *Jane Eyre*—and they would nod and quietly set to work on it, even though they seemed uncertain. I would ask them, "Do you have any questions?" but they almost never did. Yet there was a feeling of unease in the air that made me anxious, and I'm sure the same was true for them.

Then they'd leave, second period would tromp in, and I'd do the same presentation—if anything, it was a little more thorough, since I was more awake at that point—and ask if there were questions. Hands shot up.

"Is Jane in love with Mr. Rochester, or with Mr. Rochester's money?"

"Do you want *us* to develop a theme in the paper or write about how Charlotte Brontë developed a theme?"

"Is this a graded first draft?"

"Is it two pages front and back or one page front and back?"

And on and on. A dozen questions, none of which I had anticipated. By the time I answered them, the assignment was clearer to all of us. The feeling of unease dissipated, and we all went about our work much more adeptly, if not more cheerfully. With the arrival of periods three, four, and five, I once again found myself ending my assignments by asking, "Y'all have any questions?"

Crickets.

So I would say, "You know, second period asked me a really good question about this assignment, so let me tell you what I told them."

And I would just go on, answering the other questions as though they had been asked, always referring to "something second period asked."

Before the year was out, I had rearranged my lesson plans so that I gave second period the assignment first, and waited until the next day to give it to first period so they could hear the clarifications too.

Second period, man, saving everyone a lot of stress.

Eventually, of course, that school year ended, and I never had a class as helpfully inquisitive as that second period again (one of the girls from that class became a journalist, which, yes, of course!). But I kept that second period around anyway, renaming them the Other Class. I'd lecture on, let's say, Shakespeare to a class and ask for questions. When no one said, "Wait, are you saying that Shakespeare left his wife his second-best bed?" I trotted them out again. "You know," I'd say, "someone in the Other Class asked me about that bed . . ."

Whenever I pulled this trick, some quiet kid in the (real) class would lean forward, interested. They had questions, you see, but didn't ask them. There's always a bunch of kids like that in the class, I've found. The Other Class technique allows you to answer the questions they don't actually ask—because they're shy, or scared, or quiet—but that you know they have.

But 'tis not all joy and interesting facts about Shakespeare, this Other Class business. The Other Class can also help you instill pride or shame—a terrible emotion but an occasionally effective one—and function as a source of comparison. At THSB one year, I had a difficult class of sophomores. They were very chatty and occasionally quite rude. Yet they were also smart and artistic and I wanted to take them on a field trip to a Broadway show, even though I despaired that they would act so badly that someone on-stage might shush them. (I was once shushed by an actor when I was coughing in the audience at a show I attended in college, and I have never gotten over the horror of it.) So, in preparation for the show, I told them about, yes, of course, the Other Class, and how that Other Class had behaved so badly at a show that I took them to, and how the people at the theatre had given me all kinds of grief because of the Other Class. By the way, I made sure to keep this vague, implying that this was sometime in the past, since I didn't want them to think that the Other Class was just the Older Class I had the year before.

"That ain't right," one of the students said to me.

"We won't act like that," another student said.

"Babies," a third said, dismissing the Other Class. Everyone nodded in agreement.

And they were great at the show. Great on the subway. Great at the Times Square McDonald's we went to after. In fact, as we were eating, another group of students from a different school came in, and they were horrible—throwing ketchup on each other, scream- ing, ugh, they were the worst. My class and I watched them in silent scorn, until one girl turned to me and said, "They're like your *Other* Class, right, Ms. Reed?" Yep, I agreed, they sure were.

I was less deliberate in reaching for the Other Class to make students feel badly. It was instinctive. If everyone was goofing off, I might have found myself saying, "Wow, my Other Class didn't have to be told a million times to get their textbooks out." I also used the Other Class as a goad: "I think if you guys give 'The Monkey's Paw' a chance, you might like it as much as my Other Class did." And, very rarely, like this: "I'm surprised you guys are having so much trouble with *Death of a Salesman*. My Other Class loved it." Do note that this was only effective if my class could understand *Death of a Salesman* but chose not to. If they genuinely didn't get it, I was just making them feel dumb with my Other Class business.

One-on-one, I tried for kindness, and still do. One-on-thirty- four, or however many students I had that period, I tried for General Patton. I kept it moving, no matter what. After all, the Other Class could do it.

A Field Guide to Spotting Bad Teachers

Look for these signs:

- A Bad Teacher's nesting habitat is entirely covered in ungraded student papers, some from the late 1980s.
- Bad Teachers are attracted to shiny "educational" DVDs, and will spend 80 percent of the school day showing them to young people who cross their path.
- Although they share a common ancestor, Good Teachers visibly blanch when spotting Bad Teachers in the hallway and flee before the lending of lesson plans can be discussed.
- Unable to survive in the wild, Bad Teachers never volunteer to chaperone field trips, coach teams, or attend the school musical.
- Bad Teachers have several distinct cries: "Not me!" when the photocopier is jammed; "Ask her!" when a new committee chair is needed; and "Tenured!" when students complain that their US history coursework ends with the War of 1812.
- A Bad Teacher can be surprisingly long-lived—many students' parents will recall the same Bad Teacher telling the same alluvial fan jokes in the 1990s.
- Unremarkable plumage: Bad Teachers love elastic-waist pants and oversized, moth-eaten cardigans, almost always in beige.

- However, Bad Teachers are more colorful in youth: Nirvana T-shirts, jeans, Converse high-tops, vivid under-eye circles from staying up too late doing "my art" (e.g., playing in a band, writing a novel, vaping).
- Bad Teachers are completely deaf to the cries of human children.
- Bad Teachers will fake enthusiasm when confronted, such as in a parent-teacher conference, where Ashley suddenly becomes a "deeply talented student" and "there's no way I meant to give her a C; that must be a mistake!"
- Bad Teachers react with venom when startled, as when an assistant principal asks why every student in their class got a B, even Jill Weaver, who moved to Tampa in May.
- Bad Teachers can be drawn out by bait: faculty lounge birthday cake, cookies from the life skills kitchen, French Bread Pizza Day in the cafeteria.
- Bad Teachers hoard: gossip about coworkers, Post-its from the supply closet, the school's set of *A Separate Peace*, and/or wintergreen Life Savers.
- Bad Teachers are the natural predators of any student who, up until she was placed in Mr. Yang's class, liked chemistry.
- Bad Teachers are impervious to acts of aggression, including invitations to sit at the principal's table during professional development.
- When cornered by admin, Bad Teachers squawk, flap hands aggressively, and may try to lay an egg or demand the union rep.
- Delicate immune systems plague Bad Teachers: they're often the first to get the School Flu and the last to return to work after recovering.
- Bad Teachers are always on the hunt . . . for early retirement buyout offers.

Paulie

In another, better world, Paulie would have been a dancer. He was quick and muscular, compact. But in this world, Paulie was a student—well, really more the occupant of a desk—in the freshman English and theatre classes I taught during my first year at THSB.

Paulie was small and dark, in every sense of the word—dark skin, dark flashing eyes, dark soul. His teeth were strong and white, though, and we saw them a lot because he loved to laugh at us. I don't think about Paulie very often, because it pains me to do so, but when I do picture him, it's always in flashes of motion. He was so often on the run. Laughing, moving, dark: that's Paulie.

When people learn that I taught high school for eight years, they either say that I must have a lot of patience or that I must love teenagers. Neither is exactly true. I am not very patient. While I like many teenagers, I did not enter the classroom thinking I'd be hanging out with my buddies every day.

But I did try to find something to love in every kid I taught: their wit, or their kindness, or their sense of style. For some of the students I met at THSB, all I could really love was their self-confidence in the face of overwhelming odds. If I insisted that there was something to love in all my students, I almost always found it.

———

I met Paulie on the first day of school when he showed up in my fifth-period theatre class. He hadn't been there when I called roll for first period, when I had his cohort for English, but the day was so chaotic I wasn't surprised. Because there were multiple smaller schools now sharing a building that had once housed a giant high school, we couldn't use the bell system. We also lacked clocks in most every classroom, so teachers released their classes haphazardly. That first day, students had been thrust into and then yanked out of my class, mostly because Mr. Calvin hadn't scheduled them correctly, not bothering to make sure they had all their required classes. I barely registered Paulie's arrival that afternoon, trying to deal with the students openly ignoring me and my instructions. I eventually got most of the class on their feet to play a theatre game. Paulie remained seated, grinning. For the first and last time, I mistook his smile, returning it.

"Paulie, come on up! I think you'll like this game."

He said, "Theatre's for faggots."

After he laughed at my expression, I learned not to look shocked around him again, keeping my response neutral, even-keeled, no matter what. It was best not to give him the outrage he fed off of. I tried, anyway. I'm sure I didn't fool Paulie.

———

His class, 9D, was toughened by life: Patcho, a freshman seventeen-year-old father of a newborn; Nancy, whose mom was jailed for dealing drugs just days before school started that September; Samuel, who'd be arrested for robbery and sent to Rikers before the end of the semester; Ike, who met daily with his parole officer; and Alfred, who punched a hole in a wall on the third day, angry that he couldn't leave whenever he wanted.

Even though THSB was, in theory, a theatre arts magnet school, we mostly pulled in kids from the projects that abutted our building. The school was only in its second year, not old enough to have built the kind of reputation that would have drawn in theatre kids from Manhattan and other parts of Brooklyn. Every morning, our students shuffled through the scanners at security on the first floor, taking off their belts and door knocker earrings in the name of safety. It wasn't for show; there had been violent incidents at the school in a prior incarnation.

Patcho, Nancy, Samuel, Ike, Paulie, and the rest of 9D usually arrived agitated over something that had happened between their homes and my classroom door. There'd been some kind of drama, or the security guard had thrown shade, or Mr. Calvin had been cheery when cheeriness was not appropriate. I stood in my doorway to greet them.

"Hey, Patcho," I said.

"Why you always hotting me up, Ms. Reed? Come *on*."

I learned to always give in first, for the good of the class, for the dream that this would be the day when everything went well. It sort of worked too. I'd make a joke, or shrug and say "sorry," or tell them I didn't mean to hot anyone up in my whitest voice. Patcho would laugh and sit down, start on his worksheet. Samuel would give me a fist bump. Alfred would hug me. Nancy petted my hair. And Paulie? He rolled his eyes and called me "Bitch" under his breath and wouldn't sit down.

———

9D was the lower-skills cohort, the kids with lots of disabilities and emotional disorder problems. Mr. Calvin had sorted the classes that way, lumping the higher reading scores together, and the lower scores too. Whether they were actually less capable than 9A, 9B, or 9C is debatable, but they were well aware of what being in 9D meant about how the school perceived their prospects. ("There's a D in the class name," Nancy pointed out, more than once, "so . . . yeah.") That said, some members of 9D did face staggering challenges academically. Mohammed and Patcho were both approaching eighteen, when they'd be asked to move to another high school to try to graduate before they aged out of the system. There was a girl in the class, Monica, who couldn't read above a first-grade level, and a boy, DeWitt, who couldn't read, write, or even really talk at all. As for Paulie, he could read and write at a relatively high level and didn't seem to have any comprehension problems. He was, I thought, just mean.

When Mr. Calvin formally observed me teaching for the first time, bizarrely deciding to do so during the second week of school, I was pleased that the majority of the class made an attempt to complete the worksheet I specifically designed, printed up, and photocopied for the lesson (since we didn't have textbooks). Even Paulie actually sat at his desk, already remarkable. Mr. Calvin wore his usual white button-down shirt, chinos, and tie. He was the mildest-seeming theatre person I'd ever met, sitting folded up in a desk, pecking with his pencil at a clipboard. He spent a lot of time watching Paulie, while Paulie eyed him. I desperately wanted to know what either of them was thinking but was pleased that nothing untoward transpired.

In my meeting with Mr. Calvin the next day, I found out that in his opinion it had actually been a dreadful class.

"I don't want to see worksheets," Mr. Calvin said, resettling his glasses on his nose. "I want to see them up on their feet, moving around. This is a *theatre* school."

"Well, but they were learning theatre terms on that worksheet," I said. "It is only the second week of class, after all. I was trying to teach them some vocabulary so that when we do start—"

He cut me off. "No worksheets. Ever." He ran his hand down his tie and repeated, "Up on their feet."

I tried to again explain that I wanted to make sure the students knew terms like "stage right" and "offstage" and that a worksheet offered the kind of "evidence-based learning" I was required to produce by the NYCDOE to justify my grades for the class. But I saw that Mr. Calvin was definitely not interested in that. And he did have a small point: this was a lesson that could have been active. I had chosen a different way for a reason.

"Some of the kids won't participate. Paulie told me theatre's for faggots, actually," I told him.

Mr. Calvin's eyes closed and reopened slowly, a tic that I'd eventually learn to see as a deletion—he had eliminated the information he did not want to know. He waited.

I continued, "And when I can get him to join us, he gets out of control very quickly, throwing stuff, pushing the other kids. He almost bit Monica the other day. It's like he gets overexcited." I tried to explain how playing a simple theatre game had ended with Paulie lying on the floor, kicking his feet and laughing so manically, the other kids were freaked out.

"He seemed fine in class to me," Mr. Calvin said. "Maybe he just needs to be creatively engaged. Something more than worksheets. And you should be writing those incidents up on the disciplinary forms and turning them in."

"But . . ." I said, "what forms—" No one had explained anything about this to me in my nine-ish days of teaching in the NYCDOE.

"Let it be a challenge to you," he said, cutting off further questions.

———

There had been problems between Mr. Calvin and the faculty at THSB the year before, and they worsened my first year. Soon, some of the veteran teachers managed to file complaints with the UFT (the United Federation of Teachers, our union). Mr. Calvin called a faculty meeting and told us that since we saw fit to file a complaint, he had no choice but to institute a disciplinary system for the students. This was conveyed in a wounded tone, as though we too should have been appalled that it had come to this solution: a SAVE Room would be opened. (SAVE was an acronym for New York's then current school safety law.) We would now be able to send students whose behavior presented a serious disruption ("Only a *serious* disruption!" Mr. Calvin reminded us) to the SAVE Room for the remainder of the period. There was pleased murmuring among the teachers. Mr. Calvin continued to look at us sadly, shaking his head.

Although Paulie's physical behavior was terrible (running at full speed around the room, flipping chairs, going through other kids' bags, shoving stuff off desks), his real gift for disruption was his mouth, which was bad enough that the other kids, a group that used the N-word like it was a comma, were insulted by it. Paulie made many, many trips to the SAVE Room. Not just from my class. From every class. Every day. We should have put his nameplate on one of the desks in there.

One class, I was trying to help Nancy write a monologue while the rest of the class worked on writing scenes. Out of the corner of my eye I saw Patcho punch Paulie in the arm, and silently congratulated him on handling whatever problem had arisen by himself. But then there was a squeal of outrage from the other side of Paulie's desk, and Monica was on her feet, hands on her hips.

"What is wrong with you?" she said to Paulie, but her eyes snapped over to include me too. What *was* wrong with me? Why couldn't I control Paulie? I raised my eyebrows, and she pointed at him. "He called me a cunt!" she said.

"Please step into the hallway, Paulie," I said, following the latest disciplinary protocol. Mr. Calvin wanted us to try to "talk things out" with students before dismissing them to the SAVE Room.

"Nah," he said.

"Paulie," I said.

"I'll go to the SAVE Room," he said. "Write me a pass." He walked up to my desk, yanked open my desk drawer, and grabbed my stack of passes out of it. I blinked.

"Go on. Write me a pass, come on."

Trying to gather some sort of authority, I scrawled out a pass, making a note in the Remarks section about what had transpired—"Called Monica a very bad word"—and then phoned for the building's security guards, who were supposed to escort students to the SAVE Room.

"I need an escort in room 237," I said.

"This Ms. Reed?"

"Yes."

"Is it Paulie?"

". . . Yes."

"Uh-huh. We'll send someone."

But someone never appeared. Long minutes went by. Paulie whistled at the front of the room, bouncing on his toes, laughing at me. I told the class, "Ignore him," and we tried our best to do so, turning back to our work. Eventually some kids from the next class wandered in, having been let out early by their teacher, and thus 9D, including Paulie, moseyed off to their next class.

I soon learned that this was happening in all his classes. Security no longer felt it necessary to respond to the hourly calls from Paulie's teachers for escorts to the SAVE Room. They were on the first floor and we were on the third, so I guess they just got tired of doing it. There was no way to make them unless Mr. Calvin did something, and I'm sure you already know he did not. Most of his teachers stopped sending Paulie to the SAVE Room at all, but I was stubborn, determined to follow the one disciplinary procedure in place, my stay against anarchy. With Paulie in my classroom, I felt desperate, scared, even though I loomed above him and outweighed him by a hundred pounds. When he was gone, I could almost get back to what I was there for—teaching, if I possibly could, or caring, if that was all I could do.

———

In November, Paulie threw an eraser at another teacher, and the tension between Mr. Calvin and the faculty finally hit the tipping point. The union seemed like it was in the midst of what was rapidly becoming an all-out war with Mr. Calvin. Everyone could see that the union wanted the principal fired, so making the case that the school was unsafe was helpful—and Paulie was a gold mine. We were told in a union meeting to write up everything he did. I usually did that anyway, but a lot of teachers hadn't bothered. Now we were all scribbling away during every spare moment. I still have a stack of incident reports about two inches high, all about Paulie. Those incident reports about his behavior proved that Mr. Calvin's disciplinary protocol was falling apart, especially now that the security officers wouldn't get involved. Mr. Calvin wasn't guaranteeing the safety of his teachers, and those green sheets of paper were the proof.

One day I sent Paulie to the SAVE Room after he told me to "fuck off." In truth, at THSB, sending a kid to the SAVE Room for saying "fuck off" was the equivalent of expelling a kid at another school because she forgot a pencil. But I was making good progress with the other students on our Shakespeare unit, and wanted him gone before he disrupted us. He was already walking around and around the room, talking out loud to no one in particular, which had caused me to ask him to walk without talking. (He could walk! Just not talk!)

"Fuck off."

"Okay, Paulie, time for you to visit the SAVE Room."

"Good luck finding someone to take me," he said, smirking, and it was because of that smirk that I called our school office for the first time and asked for someone in administration to escort him to the SAVE Room. Mr. Calvin himself showed up, and Paulie, shocked by this turn of events, left without protest. I returned to teaching, helping Marvin with his scene.

But ten minutes later they were back at my door, Mr. Calvin with his hand on Paulie's shoulder. I had to stop teaching to step into the hallway and find out what was up.

"Paulie would like to apologize to you," Mr. Calvin told me gravely.

"What?"

"He'd like to return to your class."

"I sent him to the SAVE Room," I said. "For bad language and insubordinance." These were actual terms for actions requiring discipline, taken from the NYCDOE handbook for teachers. We new teachers were encouraged by our veteran peers to use language taken from the handbook that might act as trigger words provoking the administration's quicker response.

"Yes, but I had a talk with him," Mr. Calvin said. I saw Paulie tuck his grin away just before Mr. Calvin looked at him. "And he says he is sorry and will try to do better."

"I do not want him to return to my classroom."

"But—"

I interrupted, pushing, "He makes me feel unsafe."

"But he's *sorry*," Mr. Calvin said.

I was stuck. If I insisted that he go to the SAVE Room, I was at risk for being written up for insubordination myself. I was informed many times by my colleagues that as a teacher without tenure, I must not decline to do *anything* when directly ordered to by an administrator, or I would get written up and eventually be fired. This sounded like an Orwellian society to me, but I wasn't ready to lose my job over Paulie. So I hesitated.

"I'm so sorry," Paulie said. "I'll be a better young man."

I held the door open wider, and he slipped back in. Even as Mr. Calvin bid me adieu, I heard Marvin yelp: Paulie had done something already. I now knew not to call administration or security ever again. Welcome back, Paulie.

———

The classroom next to mine belonged to Mrs. Bay, who didn't bother to teach the math courses she was assigned. Her tenure protected her, so Mr. Calvin didn't get involved. She often slept through the morning classes, her head tucked into her arms on her desk. The sophomores who were supposed to be in her first-period class would hang out in the hallway by my door. At first I tried to get them to go to class, then I tried to get them to clear out, and after that I tried to ignore them, especially after they started making conversation with me. But they were nice to me, a lot nicer than most of my current students, so eventually I gave in and started talking to them.

"You guys should go to class," I said one day, futilely gesturing for them to get up.

"We wish we had you, Ms. Reed." This was from Bo.

"You should teach us algebra," Keysha piped up.

"I don't know anything about algebra," I protested.

A pause, and then, with a comic's timing, Keysha said: "That don't disqualify you around here." Even I laughed.

Eventually, I started opening the door for a little break in the class, especially when everyone was being ornery, or when I needed to get Paulie out. I counted on the sophomores' support. (In a school with only two classes, the sophomores were like the seniors.)

"Paulie, man, you got kicked out again? What's your problem?" Bo said one day as Paulie begrudgingly left my room, on his way to the SAVE Room. Sometimes he would go on his own, if he couldn't get any conflict started in class.

"Ms. Reed is a bitch," he responded.

"*You* a bitch, Paulie," Keysha said back. "Go to the SAVE Room."

Then she'd get to her feet to walk with him. And for once, surrounded by kids who were bigger and more numerous and even more rebellious than him, Paulie would . . . well, not cower, exactly, but give up the fight.

I'd close the door on his back, sure that they'd see that he got to the SAVE Room. At the time, this felt like a real victory.

———

A chemistry teacher, Ms. Scully, twenty-three years old and barely holding it together, told me that one of her students told her that Paulie's older brothers were drug dealers.

"How does she know that?" I asked. We were in the hallway, watching the slow, chaotic parade that was class-changing time. Since we still had no bells, it sometimes took twenty minutes to get the majority of the students into a classroom for the rest of the period.

"She lives on the same floor as them. And, get this, he's a runner for them. Takes the bags of the sugar to clients and stuff."

I sighed, as equally distressed by Ms. Scully's awkward use of the slang as I was by the news. As she talked, I watched Paulie slam a book on another kid's head.

"No, it doesn't really explain anything," I said. "Every kid here has a terrible story. I mean, almost everyone does."

She glared at me, outraged at my cruelty, as Paulie slammed the book down again, hard.

"He really needs somebody to talk to—" she began, but I was already wading into the mass of kids, telling Paulie to stop.

She wasn't wrong. But I wasn't wrong either.

———

The SAVE Room was eventually closed. The union found out about it and informed Mr. Calvin that the teachers who were staffing it were supposed to be paid for an extra period of work every day. Mr. Calvin said he didn't have money for that. In a contentious faculty meeting, he informed us that from then on, the SAVE Room was not an option. Everyone was yelling, but all I could think was "What am I going to do tomorrow when Paulie starts up?"

Despite the fact that I'd been teaching for eight years already, I was assigned a mentor teacher, a woman who would eventually disappear as well, just like the SAVE Room, after Mr. Calvin didn't pay her. But before she vanished, she observed Paulie and declared that "there's something wrong there." I was relieved to have someone agree with me, and I asked her what I should do. When I had tried to ask Mr. Calvin about the clear issues Paulie was presenting, he continued to advise trying to get Paulie engaged in my class, "up on his feet."

"He needs to be evaluated for special services," the mentor teacher said, "so you'll need his parent's permission. Start calling home."

I added a near-daily phone call home to Paulie's mom to my list of tasks. It didn't take long for her to grow tired of my attentions.

"I don't know what to do with him. When he acts bad, send him to the principal's office," she said one day. I didn't even bother to explain why that wasn't possible, or helpful. A lot of parents had no idea how school actually worked, and relied on memories from their own education ten to twenty years before, or even what they saw on TV. We routinely had to explain the existence of the required Regents tests to them.

"I really think you should consider getting him evaluated," I said, which I'd been pushing in every phone call. I wanted her to sign off on an in-school psychological evaluation for Paulie, which might allow us to get some special services for him. Or, I secretly dreamt, might get him sent to another school, one for special-ed kids, where he could finally get the help and attention he needed … while also no longer being in my class.

"He's been evaluated," she admitted one day.

"What?"

"He used to be in that special education, but I pulled him out of that because it wasn't helping."

When I reported that to my mentor, she pointed out that if Paulie had ever been in special ed, he must have been evaluated and given an IEP, an Individualized Education Plan, that should have insights into his issues and how we could best help him learn. I embarked on an attempt to find Paulie's IEP, which should have been maintained for the student's entire career in the New York City Department of Education. In talking with some of the veteran teachers, I learned that copies of *all* students' IEPs, if they had one, were supposed to be distributed to each of their teachers. We were then supposed to review them and keep them in locked desk drawers to maintain their confidentiality. But no teacher at THSB had any student's IEP. We had no idea what specific ways of reaching each student had been determined, unless the student provided some insight themselves (which some of them were perfectly capable of doing). The union filed another grievance.

In the meantime, I asked Mr. Calvin about it. He told me that he didn't distribute the IEPs because he didn't want us to "prejudge" students. I thought immediately of my hearing impairment, and how much easier it was for me to be successful in school after my parents started telling my teachers to sit me up front and repeat themselves when I didn't respond instead of assuming I was ignoring them. Didn't Paulie deserve the same? Didn't all of the kids with IEPs?

"What would happen," I asked Mr. Calvin, making it up as I went along, "if a teacher got hurt in an altercation with a student who was not receiving services for a disability?"

"That's unlikely," he snapped. "No one is going to get into an altercation with a teacher." But I'd hit a nerve. He was truly ruffled for the first time that I'd seen. I was dismissed, brusquely. For a week I worried that he was going to fire me, but instead, all teachers suddenly received copies of all of the IEPs on a Friday afternoon, distributed by Sheila, our school secretary, with a glint of triumph in her eyes. She had known all along that this was what should have been done, but Mr. Calvin had kept her from doing it.

I read Paulie's IEP and learned that in second grade, he was diagnosed with an emotional disorder. According to the IEP, he should have been in daily anger management and have a paraprofessional with him during all classes to help him stay on task and keep the other kids safe. He was also supposed to be in a special-education classroom. Although his mother had removed him from those after middle school, the rest of the IEP was still in place and had to be enforced.

So, Laura was hired as Paulie's paraprofessional. She had no prior training, but she seemed smart and tenacious. Paulie hated her on sight, and hurled abuse at her from the moment they met. Laura and I kept asking for the required anger management sessions, but Mr. Calvin said that Paulie's mother said that he didn't need them, and so long as she said that, he wasn't going to find the money in the budget for them. Laws only work if they're followed, so we didn't get Paulie everything he needed. But at least someone else was in the classroom absorbing a lot of his anger, redirecting him in a helpful way, and giving him attention.

In December, at that school talent show I told you about in the preface, Paulie told me I smelled bad. I didn't mention earlier that Patcho had been sitting beside Paulie and Marvin, and after Paulie insulted me, Patcho said, "Yeah, she smells *bad*," and slapped Paulie's hand. The last thing I heard before I ran out of the auditorium was Patcho, Paulie, and Marvin laughing. By mid-January, Paulie and Patcho seemed to have formed a friendship of sorts, which I tried to be happy about, so I put them in a group together to work on creating a scenery plan for *Fences*. When it was time for the students to present, Patcho and Paulie wouldn't shut up during Monica's group's presentation about costumes. I tried to quiet them down, but Paulie said something behind my back that caused Patcho to avoid my eyes and groan, "Ohhhh, mannnn." I steeled myself not to respond, but suddenly Monica was up and yelling at Paulie.

"You need to back off! Just shut up while we presenting!"

"Oooh," Paulie said, elbowing Patcho, overjoyed that he had really set her off this time.

"Shut up!" Monica said. "She a good teacher!"

It took me a long minute to realize Monica was defending me. I was shocked. It wasn't the first fight I'd seen or broken up in my classroom, and it wasn't even the first time 9D got into it, but it was the first time that I seemed to be the catalyst for the fight. Laura was out that day, and Mr. Calvin never bothered to get a substitute for her, saving the money, so I was the only adult around when it all went to hell.

"What you gonna do?" Paulie asked mockingly. Monica took a swing at him. He was momentarily surprised—for once, his words had provoked an actual, physical reaction—and then his eyes narrowed and he leapt toward her. They were on the floor in seconds, pummeling each other.

I yelled at the other girls to drag Monica into the hallway, and Patcho tried to hold back Paulie, who was thrashing and screaming. I was on the phone to security, calmly informing them it was a real fight, yes, I really did need them. Now, please. "Yes, room 237, and yes, Paulie." At the same time, Nancy went to the door and yelled, "WE NEED HELP!"

A few seconds later, two security guards came running from one direction and Mr. Calvin from another. The girls had been holding Monica back, so I took over gently pinning her against the wall, knowing that so long as she had to shove me to get free, she wasn't going to do it. But she was still halfheartedly squirming and screaming profanities at Paulie. Meanwhile, Mr. Calvin locked his arms around Paulie's chest from behind, even though the boy was kicking so hard that his feet barely touched the floor. Mr. Calvin yelled at the security officers to leave, that he had it all under control. "We're fine!" he said to them. They looked at me, shrugged in solidarity, and left. Monica stilled, interested in seeing what was going to happen, as Paulie continued to thrash.

"Paulie! It's me! Mr. Calvin! Your principal!" Mr. Calvin cried.

Paulie stilled, then took a moment to look back at him in disgust. "What the fuck, *my* principal?" he said. "You let go of me, you cracker piece of shit!" Then he kicked Mr. Calvin in the shin.

I didn't actually see that part, as I had turned away to check on the other kids. But I heard him say something, and we all winced at the crack of his foot connecting with Mr. Calvin's leg, the sound drawing a reflexive "Ohhh, shiiiiitttt" from several students. Patcho, who was reliable on details, told me about it later.

Mr. Calvin dropped to the floor, clutching his leg. Paulie took off running, the now returning security officers tackling him at the entrance to the stairwell. And in a matter of moments they were all gone—guards, Paulie, Mr. Calvin, Mr. Calvin's pride—a parade of motion down the hallway to Mr. Calvin's office, where various punishments would be handed out and, I assumed, an ice pack for his leg would be fetched. I turned back to my classroom, shaking, the rest of the kids watching, some of them still holding the sketches for their presentations. I silently led them back into the room and sat behind my desk while they took their seats.

"We're all upset," I said. "Is it okay if we just sit quietly for the rest of the period?" They agreed that this was a good idea. We sat, staring off into space, taking deep breaths, thinking, for the next twenty minutes, in a completely silent classroom. It was the quietest we'd ever been.

———

Monica got a two-day suspension and didn't complain, telling me it was worth it to get to finally punch Paulie.

"I can't believe I didn't do that before," she said when she returned to class.

"Me either," I said, before I could stop myself.

"It felt good," she said. I nodded. I knew it had.

After that, Mr. Calvin decided that he hated Paulie and wanted him out of the school. Funny thing, though: all of the paperwork we teachers had turned in—the anecdotal reports, the safety violations—couldn't be found, so he didn't have anything to build a case on, since the rest of the class pretended that they hadn't seen anything. They all hated Mr. Calvin more than they wanted to see Paulie gone. Paulie ended up being suspended for a week, a puny punishment indeed, but all that could be assigned for a first demeanor. Mr. Calvin had never taken any of his many transgressions seriously enough to suspend him for very long before.

The faculty was now urged to keep voluminous paperwork on even the mildest of Paulie's infractions. After a few weeks of that, with a stack of anecdotals at his disposal, Mr. Calvin called in Paulie's mother. For reasons I never really grasped, I was pulled out of teaching a class to attend this meeting, in which Mr. Calvin told her she needed to find another school for Paulie. To my surprise, she appeared to be a perfectly normal woman, wearing jeans, an Ed Hardy T-shirt, and the kind of quilted vest my mom owns. I don't know what I was expecting, but it certainly wasn't someone who seemed to be entirely together.

"I don't see what the problem is," she said. "The only person who ever complains to me is Miss Reed here, so why don't you just put him in another class since she can't handle him?"

For once, I was smart enough to keep my mouth shut. He was indeed too much for me! Paulie was moved to Ms. Scully's classes. Her sympathy for him didn't last very long, and she wrote up many reports for Paulie's file.

One day I heard wails from the hallway. The sophomore girls hanging out in my classroom during a free period and I went out to investigate, finding Ms. Scully slumped almost on the hallway floor, sobbing. It turned out that Paulie told her that he knows she likes to eat her students' pussies. When we heard that, the girls and I made the exact same teeth-sucking sound of displeasure, and then we comforted her.

This incident—and Ms. Scully's subsequent avowals that she felt unsafe—allowed Mr. Calvin to put Paulie on Superintendent's Suspension, and thus he spent the remaining few months of the school year in another school on the other side of Brooklyn. The mood at THSB was immediately noticeably lighter, and 9D's work improved—nothing miraculous, but they had real moments of actual learning.

When Paulie came back in the fall of the next year, Mr. Calvin did not. We had a new principal who managed to get Paulie transferred to another high school against his mother's will. But Paulie showed up again at THSB a few months later. Once the school he transferred to realized what kind of kid they had accepted, they conveniently lost the transfer paperwork and sent him back to us. This kind of thing, a principal's con followed by another principal's con, apparently happened all the time, as kids like Paulie got shuffled around the system, no one wanting to take them on. He was soon back in Ms. Scully's class as well as the other freshman-level classes, since he hadn't passed a single course. The new freshmen were entirely unimpressed by Paulie—where 9D saw him as an equal, they saw him as a massive loser, and this deflated him, as did the threat of actual discipline. He could no longer con Mr. Calvin into letting him back into the classroom. The new principal, full of faults as he was, didn't try to reason with Paulie and made it clear he was on his way out. (He also got us clocks. We never did get bells.)

Finally, Paulie was somehow forced to go to another school. I don't know the details, as I was teaching Keysha and Bo's class by then (it turned out that they were great students when they had a teacher who bothered to teach). Whatever happened, he was truly transferred, never to return, gone from all of our lives. But before he left, Paulie decided to make a tour of the school to say goodbye to all his old teachers. I do think he was actually a little sad. He showed up at my door without warning one afternoon.

"Bye, Ms. Reed. I'm leaving THSB."

"Good luck, Paulie," I said. "I hope you'll like your new school bet—" But he had already left my classroom, the door slamming in my face before I could finish the sentence.

As I rode the subway home that day, I knew I should be sad at the state of the whole situation and what it said about poverty, and disability, and racism, and privilege. And I suppose I was intellectually sad, if that's possible. But in my gut, I felt relieved.

I also realized that I never did find anything to love about Paulie. That was the real challenge to me, and I failed at it. I still feel guilty about it, and, to be frank, I think I should.

———

The year that I had Paulie, I taught another cohort of freshmen too, 9A. They were the kids who tested better, had higher scores. They were far more self-satisfied about their scholastic gifts than any group of ninth graders who mostly couldn't read above a sixth-grade level should be, and they didn't like me at first because I pushed them to do even better. Eventually we mostly worked things out, but at first, whew, it was not easy going.

Once, I walked in from my lunch to find that someone from 9A had scrawled "Ms. Reed is a Fat Hoe" on one of my posters. I lectured 9A about it, trying to get someone to fess up, which didn't happen, and then I was upset enough about it that I showed it to 9D when they came in for the next class, telling them that it really hurt my feelings.

"That's stupid," Paulie said. "You got a big booty for a white lady, but you ain't fat."

I recognize that there's nothing in that sentence that's a compliment, exactly, but it was the nicest thing that Paulie ever said to me, and the only real glimpse I got of him as a person who wasn't horrible through and through, a kid with some sense of fairness. Perhaps for that reason, I give it the weight of truth. And to be honest, every time I think of it, I laugh.

It's Your Twenty-Minute Lunch Period!

Host: Welcome back, everyone! It's time for another round of our game! As you know, every week we see if our teacher contestant can . . . what?

Audience: EAT THEIR LUNCH!

Host: That's right! They have twenty minutes, so surely they'll be able to eat lunch, right?

Audience cackles.

Host: But, of course, they'll have to dodge our interruptions to do it. Hey, audience, so far, in our five years on the air, how many teachers have actually eaten their lunch in the time allotted and thus won our game?

Audience: (*chanting*) ZERO! ZERO! ZERO!

Host: Well, there's always a first time! (*He joins the audience in their dismissive laughter.*) Just a reminder of our rules: the contestant must eat their entire lunch, *while sitting down*, and they must finish *before the bell rings*! Okay, let's give a big welcome to our contestant this week, Yolanda Hayer, who teaches—wait, what kind of teacher are you, Yolanda?

Yolanda has entered, carrying a brown bag lunch.

Yolanda: I'm dual-certified in secondary math and French.

Host: And what are you teaching now?

Yolanda: High school band.

Host: That sounds about right. All right, Yolanda, are you ready? Go!

Yolanda races to a chair and desk, sits down, and opens her bag. Just as she's about to bite into her sandwich, the classroom door is flung open. It's another teacher, Harriet.

Harriet: Yolanda! A few of us are walking over to Subway, wanna come?

Yolanda hesitates.

Audience: (*chanting*) You should go! You have enough time! A hot lunch would taste good!

Host: Oh, no, Yolanda, what are you going to choose? You know that Subway has those cookies—they don't taste like anything, but still, cookies!

Yolanda: Well . . . I— No! No, thank you. I brought my lunch.

Harriet shrugs at the audience and leaves.

Host: Very impressive, Yolanda! You have eighteen minutes left to eat your lunch.

Again, Yolanda is about to take a bite when the door is flung open by Benny, a student.

Benny: Ms. Hayer, did I leave my retainer in here? It costs, like, a thousand dollars, and my mom will kill me if I lost it again.

Yolanda: Well, take a look around.

She takes one bite of her sandwich. Benny looks around halfheartedly, winks at the audience, and begins to cry. Yolanda takes another bite. He cries more audibly.

Yolanda: Oh, Benny, what's wrong?

Benny: It's just that my mom says if I keep losing stuff, it means I'm not responsible enough to go to college, and I don't want to have to live at home forever because my sister is into K-pop now, and…

Yolanda abandons her desk and puts her arm around Benny, comforting him. The audience snickers.

Host: Oh, no, Yolanda, you got what?

Audience: (*chanting*) SUCKERED! SUCKERED! SUCKERED!

Host: If we fast-forward through this interruption, it turns out that Benny just wanted to get out of gym! He doesn't even wear a retainer! You lost ten minutes for no reason! You only have eight minutes left!

As Benny leaves, laughing, Yolanda returns to her desk and shoves the sandwich into her mouth. She eats as rapidly as possible. There is a knock on her door, then it opens to reveal Guadalupe, the school secretary.

Guadalupe: Yo-Yo, I'm so sorry to ask you this, but the copier jammed again, and you're the only one who can fix it, could you—

Reluctantly but firmly, Yolanda shakes her head. Guadalupe shrugs at the audience, who boo, and exits. The door is opened again. This time, it's Bridget, holding a flyer.

Bridget: Ms. Hayer, my brother is selling different kinds of cheesecakes for the Boy Scouts, and you said when I was selling different kinds of Bundt cakes for my sister for the Girls Scouts that I should come back another time, so I wanted to know, do you want to buy a cheesecake? They have something called Band Teacher's Delight. Or there are fifty-five other choices.

Yolanda hesitates.

Audience: (*chanting*) CHEESEcake! CHEESEcake! CHEESEcake!

Yolanda: Bridget, honey, come back at the end of the day, okay?

Vanquished, Bridget nods and departs. More booing. Yolanda has finished the sandwich. She holds the empty sandwich bag up triumphantly.

Host: Congratulations, Yolanda! With five minutes left, you finished the main portion of the meal! But you were a little ambitious this morning, so—well, go ahead and unpack the rest of the lunch bag.

Yolanda takes out a yogurt, a small bag of chips, and a cookie. She drops them on her desk and puts her head in her hands.

Yolanda: Good Lord, where do I think I work?

Just then, there is a knock at the door. It's Bert, the assistant principal, and he walks right in, taking a seat on Yolanda's desk, blocking her from reaching her lunch.

Bert: Ms. Hayer! I wanted to talk to you about buying new instruments for the band. How do you feel about putting together a fund-raiser? We'll need about ten thousand dollars, I think, give or take five thousand dollars. What about selling cheesecakes? You would need to sell fifty thousand cheesecakes, which seems reasonable, right?

But the audience hisses—Yolanda has managed to get the bag of chips and is chowing down.

Host: Uh-oh, with three minutes left, it's time to go into our lightning round!

The door flies open. It's Guadalupe again.

Guadalupe: So sorry, Yo-Yo, but I just wanted to let you know that Mr. Abdul spilled coffee on that sheet music you copied during your free period, so you have no lesson plan for the class that starts in five minutes.

But Yolanda has grabbed the yogurt and is shotgunning it.

Yolanda: It's okay! We'll review the videotape of last week's concert!

Clyde, the school janitor, appears in the doorway.

Clyde: Yolanda, sucks, but a kid just threw up all over the video cabinet in the band room. See ya!

Host: Two minutes left!

The audience is silent, nervous.

Yolanda: (*as she grabs the cookie*) We'll make up our own songs! The class is now about *jazz*!

Everyone else reacts in begrudging admiration.

Bert: I don't know, you guys, this one is a real pro!

Host: She certainly is, and she's given us a real run for the money, but we have one more trick up our sleeve . . .

Audience: (*chanting*) Fire DRILL! Fire DRILL!

A loud alarm begins blaring.

Bert: Ah-ha! Well, it looks like we'll have to step out—

Yolanda: (*desperately*) I'll just wait here! It's probably not real! It never is!

Guadalupe: I don't know, there was a story on Yahoo! News about this teacher who didn't follow fire drill protocol and the school hamster, Pepperpot, died.

Audience: AWWWWWW!

Yolanda: (*through a mouthful of cookie*) We don't have a hamster!

Bert: Ms. Hayer, I know you wouldn't want to countermand a direct order—

Yolanda: I'm DONE!

She waves the empty brown bag. The alarm stops. Silence. Bert, Guadalupe, Clyde, Bridget, Benny, and Harriet gather off to one side, muttering.

Yolanda: Did you hear me? I'm done! (*She turns to the audience.*) HA HA HA! I did it! I ate my whole lunch, seated at my desk, during my lunch period!

Host: Congratulations, Yolanda. You are our first winner. I'm shocked, to be honest. But your determination, utter focus, and willingness to abandon your students and colleagues made it happen. Brava to you!

Yolanda: Thank you! What do I win?

Host: Well, you've already won it! You got to eat your entire lunch!

Yolanda: That's it? I don't win money for DonorsChoose or stuff for my classroom or anything?

Host: Oh, no. That's it, except for a case of indigestion. (*He turns to the audience.*) Sure, the teacher won this time, but don't give up hope, audience! Time is on our side, and next week, we're introducing a new concept we like to call . . . Spills!

The audience revives, begins to cheer.

Host: We'll see you next week for another round of *It's Your Twenty-Minute Lunch Period!* Bye-bye, folks!

As the credits roll, we hear . . .

Yolanda: Guadalupe, are you mad at me?

To Stan, with Love

Dear Stan,

I think you'd be surprised how often I think about you. I mean, I was just your teacher, not your parent, or girlfriend, or even your friend, really. I hope they think about you every day. I bet they do. You were deeply loved.

You and me, we didn't have much of a bond. We fought most of the time, as I recall. Okay, "fight" is too strong a word, but let's be honest, which I think you usually were: we were not fans of each other. You didn't like school, so you were rude to me. I really wanted to help you learn, but oh, you wore me down, just having to constantly, constantly ask you to participate or at least not distract. Sometimes you wouldn't come to school, or at least to my class, for a while. Then you'd be back, grinning that million-dollar smile, flirting with the girls, and brushing your hair, sitting off to the side, paying me no attention.

But you were impressed the day I came in with a new iPhone. That I had continued to use my sad little BlackBerry, which I loved, grieved you deeply, and you nagged me more than once to get a better phone. I wish I had told you the truth—that I couldn't afford to upgrade it for a long time. I think we should have talked about things like this more often. I worry that each of you, the students, felt you were alone in your financial woes. Anyway, one day the BlackBerry broke, and I upgraded—and you were so proud of me! I remember you lecturing me about getting a good case for the iPhone, something sturdy that would protect it.

People said you were in a gang, but that was said about every boy in the school, practically. It's not that I didn't think it was true, it's just that I didn't know what to do if it was. Like many people, I found it hard to believe that someone with whom I'd had so many benign everyday interactions could also be violent. Besides, I had to maintain my authority in my classroom, and I found that easier to do if I just never, ever thought about what any of you did in the dark.

Something changed for you just before you died. I don't know what it was for sure. I heard that your girlfriend told you she was pregnant, and you were gobsmacked. If so, that makes sense—realizing you're about to become a father could make you feel a little more serious about things, make you want a good education. I always tried to get you to do the work for my class, but I didn't expect much. One day, though, you asked me a clarifying question about the essay I'd asked everybody to write. I played it cool, but inside I was pumping my fist, hugging you, waving to the cheering crowd: YOU. WERE. ENGAGED AND LEARNING.

Not too long after that, we fell into conversation after class. I think it was on a Monday or a Tuesday. I was teaching Careers in the Arts at that point, a class I wasn't qualified to lead—Ms. Giglio was supposed to teach it, but the new principal messed up her schedule and it got dumped on me just before the semester began with only a day or so to prepare. But the one nice thing about teaching it was that students sometimes turned to me for career advice, which is what you did that day. You told me you were thinking of going into carpentry. I told you that was a good job, that working with your hands can be fulfilling, and the pay was good if you got into a union.

You asked me if the pay would be enough to support a family. I said I thought so. You smiled that smile and left. That was the last time I would talk to you.

I don't remember if you came to class the next few days, but for some reason, I think you might not have. Maybe the events that would end your life were set in motion on that Wednesday or Thursday. I don't know. In any case, you were in school on Friday and you turned in your homework for the first time, which thrilled me. The rest of the day went on as usual. It was sunny out, for October. Summer can really linger on and on in Brooklyn, and it did that year. When I taught my last period that day, your classmates were like horses at the bit, inching, inching, to get out of there and into the weekend.

In the time it took me to say goodbye to that class, putter around my room a bit, and wander down to the school office to wait for instructions on how I could help with the performance of the school play that night, you died. A car had driven up on the street outside our school, someone had lowered a gun at you, and you had been shot in the face. A couple of other students were hit too. In those few minutes.

It bothers me that they were unremarkable minutes for me, that I didn't even hear the gunshots. School had just let out—you and your friends and classmates were out on the avenue, on your way home, hanging out, going to McDonald's, whatever you did when the freedom of the weekend had finally arrived. And then everything changed.

I understand that time is not flexible, and that we cannot go back and replay events to end differently. Yet I almost always think, when I think of you, that I should have asked you to stop by to talk more about your career plans. It had occurred to me to suggest you apprentice at a union. I could have told you that. I should have gone out into the hall and bumped fists and high-fived you guys as you left. Maybe I would have slowed you down enough that they didn't find you. I'm sure every teacher, every adult, maybe everyone at our school feels this way.

You'd be shocked at how much it affected us, how word went around. I found out when Ms. Lorraine came in, shaken and crying. "Stan is dead!" she screamed. We stared, stammered out questions. "He's been shot dead!" she said.

So much happened after that, so many people tried to help, but you were already dead. Ms. Lorraine ran back into the hallway to tell other people. Mr. Marc went running out of the office to get to you. We suddenly realized that the police lights and sirens were not the everyday chaos of New York but were specifically there for you and the other students who were shot, who would survive. In shock, I headed to the library, where the drama kids were. Ms. Duffy and Ms. Giglio were there. We hugged, and began to gather whoever was around.

Stan, I wish you could have seen how upset everyone was. I think you knew you were loved—you joined a gang for the money, I think, not the camaraderie—but you would have been astounded. Deirdre cried so hard for you. I held her and let her cry for over fifteen minutes. That room was full of sobbing for hours. Other people wanted revenge, to shoot those who had shot you. A lot of people sat in shock, some who knew you, some who didn't. A lot of us, maybe all of us, were scared. The police wouldn't let us leave, but after a couple of hours they let the Domino's across the street deliver pizza to us, so that's what we ate while we waited.

Enough time went by that a news website published a picture of your body, dead or dying, part of a story that my friends texted or emailed or called to tell me not to look at. But I did. You had crumpled; you, to whom appearance and pride meant so much, had no dignity in your last moments. I'm sorry. Anyone deserves better. You certainly did.

We had a weak principal that year. I know you didn't respect her. You were shot in mid-October, and she'd only been on the job since mid-August. She didn't know how to work at a school like ours, and she wasn't a strong person. She stepped aside, helpless, and her bosses stepped in. The school brought in counselors (for the students, not the teachers) on Monday. We posted a beautiful mural Jeffrey made for you, and we signed it. When we came back to class for real on Tuesday or Wednesday, we looked at the desk where you had sat, and after a long, long, hard silence, the longest I've ever heard in my classroom, we talked about you. One of my classes, from your grade, dedicated the play we wrote to you. It was my idea. It was something, but it wasn't nearly enough.

The kids who got shot had to be transferred to other schools for their safety. Your class never recovered. We teachers were left to get through it on our own. The principal didn't get any better. The police have a surveillance video of your killer, but they've never arrested him. Maybe they don't know who he is, I don't know. Your death seems somehow both unnoticed and deeply traumatic. It changed me. It broke my heart.

———

But that was all to come. I didn't cry that Friday, not until I was packing up my bag to go home, after the police said that it was okay for us to leave, after most of the kids had been picked up by their parents, after Ms. Giglio said she would drive me and Ms. Duffy home so we didn't have to wait at the deserted bus stop in a neighborhood where our student had been killed. I looked in my bag and saw that I had the folder with your homework to grade. That's when I cried.

It's been eight years. Sometimes I think about how old you'd be now, what your life would be like if you were alive. Like I said, I truly didn't know you well, so I have no real insight. No teacher wants to outlive her students. Why am I, rapidly aging, prone to defensiveness, inordinately fond of dessert, still chugging along in my midforties, and you remain dead at, always, sixteen? Why do the things you left behind still exist, but you are gone?

I graded your homework. I didn't know what else to do with it. You got a B. It was the highest grade you'd earned in my class thus far. So, I guess, ever.

That's all I wanted to tell you, except to let you know that every time I looked at my iPhone, I thought of you and what you said. But I didn't buy a good case. I thought it would cost too much. I broke that phone within a few months by dropping it on the sidewalk, and then I went on to break an iPhone just about once a year for the next three years, until finally I bought a good case for it, like you told me to. That iPhone lasted me until just a few weeks ago, when it finally died on my forty-fifth birthday, which I spent in Brooklyn. It was a sunny day. I walked to the store I knew in Park Slope and upgraded to the best iPhone I could afford, and bought a sturdy case for it too. I thought of you.

With love,
Ms. Reed

Field Trip Rules

Dear Students:

As you know, after what happened during what's become known as the *Les Mis* Clap-Along Incident, I've been reluctant to escort another THSB class on a field trip to a Broadway show. However, we were recently given free tickets to see the revival of *Godspell* at Circle in the Square, starring Corbin Bleu, whom I have never, ever heard of, but who I am reliably told is "that hottie from *High School Musical*." Because we truly cannot endure any more begging, and because we love *Godspell*, Ms. Giglio, Ms. Duffy, and I have agreed to chaperone this trip. Even better, we have somehow managed to get the DOE bus department website to work, and have secured a school bus to take us to and from the show. Huzzah! So many miracles. It truly is . . . God's spell.

Here are our expectations and rules:

1. All students must wear actual pants to the show. Not leggings. Pants.
   a. Skirts over leggings are fine.
      i. This goes for boys too.
2. We will leave after second period.

    a. Yes, that means you have to attend the first two periods.

       i. Yes, even if you have an algebra test.

       ii. Well, if you try coming in late, you won't go on the trip, because we will be around to your first period classes to make sure you're there, because that is the kind of extra your theatre teachers are.

3. You can and should bring your phones and headphones on the bus, but you may not listen to music anywhere else. It does not make sense to go to a musical and listen to different music during that musical, y'all.

    a. It also does not make sense—in fact, it makes even less sense—to listen to music from a musical while at a performance of that musical. Just watch and listen to the show!

4. We're going to Shake Shack to eat beforehand. Bring money for lunch.

    a. We know McDonald's is cheaper. We're still going to Shake Shack. There's a McDonald's across the street, if you insist on going there.

    b. If you want to bring a packed lunch, you can. We can also get you a packed lunch from the cafeteria if you let us know.

    c. No, you're not allowed to take the subway twenty blocks uptown to eat at that cool Vietnamese place you went to with your older sister that one time. We don't care how sure you are you can make it back by the curtain.

    d. You may not bring the rest of your food or drink into the theatre. If you try to do this and an usher catches you and kicks you out, we are not intervening. #ShowsBeforeBros

5. Appropriate audience behavior is required. Clapping, mild "whoo!"-ing after a big number, gentle weeping, sighs of satisfaction, and the occasional "Awww!" are fine.

   a. Do not yell out "Go *on*, Jesus! YOU CAN GET IT!"

   b. Do not ask any cast member for their phone number, before, during, or after the show.

   c. Do not offer to sing harmony on "Day by Day."

   d. If there is audience participation, do not try to get them to pick Dwight; you know he doesn't like it.

   e. For the love of God, stop clapping along when the song is over. It's not a hockey game.

   f. If we meet any of the cast after the show, please remember 5b.

6. There is a very high likelihood that Ms. Reed will cry during "Prepare Ye," "Day by Day," and also every other song. You are not allowed to tease her.

7. We will have a discussion about the show on the way home. That is the appropriate time to bring up whether John the Baptist is skanky or not. Do not bring up the skankiness of any character until we are on the bus, headed home.

   a. If you have notes for the costume, set, lighting, or sound designer, please also hold those for the bus ride home.

   b. If you fail to follow this rule, you will be asked to write up your thoughts in a five-page paper that we will forward to the appropriate person.

8. You may purchase souvenirs if you like. Please do not ask your teachers to help you purchase them. As we have told you, none of the three of us grew up wealthy, and we went without T-shirts from any Broadway shows we saw at your age. We all survived just fine into adulthood.

a. Ms. Reed is a full-grown woman and if she wants to spend $50 on a *Godspell* sweatshirt, she is allowed. Someday you will be full-grown and you will attend yet another revival of *Godspell*, and you can buy yourself a sweatshirt.

9. At no time will the singing of "99 Bottles of Beer on the Wall" be allowed, but especially not if we are caught in rush-hour traffic on the BQE.

10. Even if we drive directly by a really dope sneaker shop, we are not going to stop. You can take a note of where it is and get your parents to take you on a weekend. Just to reiterate: We are not stopping to shop for sneakers.

11. We will arrive back to the school in time for evening rehearsal, and Ms. Duffy says she will order pizza if you've behaved well. So, please remember: Good behavior = Pizza!

12. Be kind, have fun, and whatever you do, do not sit on the sidewalk in Manhattan, for there be staph infections.

Broadway, ho! See you at 10 A.M. on the 25th!

Teachers Reveal the Holiday Gifts They Actually Want

Mrs. Mitchell, Preschool Teacher: "One solid hour of absolute quiet every day from five to six P.M."

Mr. Nelson, High School Science Teacher: "To be able to teach about the solar system without someone yelling, 'No, *your* anus!!!' from the back row."

Mrs. McAdams, High School Nurse: "Five hundred boxes of tampons."

Ms. Simpson, Sixth-Grade Teacher: "World peace, a new pencil sharpener, and a complete set of the Harry Potter books that magically return to my bookshelves two weeks after being borrowed."

Mr. Steinberg, High School Algebra Teacher: "That just once someone would give me a Hanukkah card instead of a Christmas card."

Mr. Brown, Fourth-Grade Teacher: "Please get the class moms to stop flirting with me. I am very gay."

Ms. Drury, High School English Teacher: "A gift card is fine. To where? Anywhere. Or cash. Cash is good. In an envelope? I mean, sure, if you feel that classes it up."

Ms. DuPré, High School Spanish Teacher: "Is it possible to teach the entire world how to roll their Rs? Because I'd like that, a lot."

Ms. Stephens, Second-Grade Teacher: "That 'Baby Shark' would forever disappear from our collective consciousness."

Ms. Amir, High School Social Studies Teacher: "It would be great if I could have a complete set of posters with the US Constitution, the Bill of Rights, the Declaration of Independence, and the lyrics to Beyoncé's 'Formation' for the classroom!"

Miss Susan, Kindergarten Teacher: "No school on Fridays? Or that kindergarten gets out an hour earlier than the rest of the school every day? Either one would be fine."

Ms. Delaney, First-Grade Teacher: "It's my first year of teaching, so I'd love a memento from my class. Maybe a painting with all their handprints on it? That would be so special!"

Mrs. Binghampton, High School English Teacher: "Something my students make for me themselves. Ha! No, I'm kidding. A Starbucks gift card. For two hundred dollars."

Mrs. Stewart, High School Math Teacher: "You're sweet to ask, but I'm retiring at the end of the year, and I have 134 sick days saved up, so my holiday gift is not returning to school after Thanksgiving."

I'm Going to Make It through the Last Faculty Meeting of the Year by "Yes, and . . ."-ing It

The meeting will be scheduled for 7 A.M.

Yes, and I will be wide awake at 4 A.M., convinced I was late and unable to fall back asleep.

Yes, and the meeting will be held in the only classroom in the school without windows.

Yes, and it will start fifteen minutes late.

Yes, and I will have arrived at the meeting ten minutes early, even though I know it will start late, because I have been at the school since 6:15 A.M.

Yes, and the coffee shop will not have been able to make my usual, because they opened mere seconds before I arrived.

Yes, and I will drink this mistake matcha pineapple latte that they gave me half off anyway because, caffeine.

Yes, and it will turn out that Gary, the principal, bought donuts and coffee for everyone anyway, since it's the last faculty meeting of the year.

Yes, and I will only learn about that when Bev sits down next to me at 7:13, crowing about getting the last donut even though "I am running soooo late!" because it will turn out that Gary set up the donuts and coffee at the back of the classroom five minutes after the meeting was supposed to start.

Yes, and he announced that he brought coffee and donuts, but it's possible I was taking a micro-nap and missed that.

Yes, and Bev has 467 saved sick days because she's been a teacher for thirty years and never gets ill, yet she still showed up for this meeting.

Yes, and I end up with a half cup of coffee, but at least it's not pineapple-y.

Yes, and the first topic of discussion at the meeting is next year's curriculum.

Yes, and Bev, the school's gym teacher, will yell, "Volleyball again!" and Natalie, the school's French teacher, will say, "French!" and they will laugh, then high-five.

Yes, and Gary will ask who wants to head up the curriculum committee that will meet three times over the summer, but only for four hours at a time and always on Fridays in the un-air-conditioned school.

Yes, and I don't have tenure, so I will volunteer.

Yes, and Bev will say, "Couldn't pay me to do it, I'll be in the Outer Banks!"

Yes, and Natalie will say, "Please, they're not paying anyone."

Yes, and I will sit on my hands to keep from slapping both of them when they high-five again.

Yes, and Gary will then tell us we have a special visitor today who will be leading the professional development portion of the meeting, but before we get started we need to stand up and "shake out the tired."

Yes, and I will watch my colleagues, all of whom have at least two college degrees, begrudgingly bounce on their heels while Gary walks around the room clapping.

Yes, and when Gary gets close to me, I will also bounce and energetically swing my arms, which causes me to knock over the latte, so at least I don't feel guilty about not drinking it anymore, plus I get to leave to grab some paper towels.

Yes, and in the bathroom I'll run into what appears to be a twelve-year-old girl in a business suit, telling herself, "This is YOUR fight song!" in the mirror.

Yes, and when I return to the meeting I'll realize that the twelve-year-old is our professional development leader, and that she's also Gary's adult daughter, Bethany. She will inform us that she's here to share what she learned from her student teaching assignment at a Waldorf/Montessori preschool. Bethany will then tell us to hug ourselves and then hug someone near us, and to tell ourselves and the other person, "You are doing the best you can."

Yes, and I'll learn that Bev smells like a not-unintriguing mix of weed, sweat, cat litter, and Elizabeth Arden's Red Door.

Yes, and Bev will tell me, "You are doing . . . wait, what was it?" And I'll say, "The best I can?" And Bev will say, "Sure, that," and sit back down.

Yes, and then Bethany will start to hand out crayons, telling us to take our favorite color, and I'll take gray, even though it's not my favorite color, until someone in the back of the room says, "Hell, no."

Yes, and Bethany will freeze and look to Gary, who will stand up and cross his arms and look meaningfully around the room, and just as he's about to sit back down, the same voice will say, "I have tenure, my dude, no goddamn crayons."

Yes, and Bethany will burst into tears and run out of the room.

Yes, and Gary will run after her, yelling at the assistant principal, inexplicably always called Mrs. Griffith, to start her presentation on our new discipline system called AROWBOAT.

Yes, and Mrs. Griffith will ask if "a science teacher" will come up and help her set up the PowerPoint.

Yes, and no one will budge, including me. I teach math.

Yes, and the bell will ring, signaling that students will arrive in five minutes.

Yes, and everyone will leap to their feet, papers and coffee cups and donuts flying, as we make a mad dash to get to the photocopier first.

Yes, and I will realize that I should have used the spare forty-five early-morning minutes I had here at school to make the 120 copies of the special famous lady mathematicians worksheet that I need today.

Yes, and in that moment when I stand in the classroom completely stunned, Mrs. Griffith will come over and ask me if I wouldn't mind making copies of her five-page handout—front and back—about how AROWBOAT connects to the Common Core curriculum.

Yes, and I will agree, because I don't have tenure.

Yes, and in the hallway Bev will hiss at me, "You shouldn't do that stuff for them."

Yes, and I'll say, "Yes, and . . ." but Bev will already be heading down the stairs, and the last week of school has begun.

Part III

College

All Part of a Plan, Maybe; or, How I Came to Be a Professor

In 1928, Thornton Wilder's second novel, *The Bridge of San Luis Rey*, won the Pulitzer Prize in Fiction. As a Wilder fanatic, I've read it several times, and it perplexes me, which I think he wanted, since he very often left readers pondering, as befits a long career of writing about religious and spiritual matters. *The Bridge of San Luis Rey* is set in eighteenth-century Peru and tells the story of a friar who happens to be waiting to cross a rope bridge over a canyon when it collapses with five people on it, sending them all plunging to their deaths. The monk is deeply affected by this, and decides to try to collect as much information as he can about the five victims, in hopes of proving definitively that God does (or does not!) have a plan for each life.

At the end of the tale, it's revealed—ahem, nearly one-hundred-year-old spoiler—that the friar's work was found to be heretical by church authorities and both it and he were burned. The novel closes with what has become one of Wilder's most famous quotes: "There is a land of the living and a land of the dead, and the bridge is love, the only survival, the only meaning." In this way, Wilder leaves the ending ambiguous, and powerful. The friar's initial proposition—"Either we live by accident and die by accident, or we live by plan and die by plan"—isn't resolved. That's the ambiguity, and that's what's stayed with me.

Look, I have no more idea than anyone else which it is. Both options give me the willies: How dare I blithely declare that an innocent child's death is part of a plan? Or that the tornado that leveled a town is God's will? But the trajectory of my own life doesn't feel accidental either: Why did Geri call me for an interview without my ever sending her my résumé? Why did the guy who was given a full scholarship to the MFA program at Pitt decide to go elsewhere, so that I, the writing program's second choice, ended up at the school that's been my home ever since? Like a basic cable commercial for a local psychic, I have to ask: Was this coincidence, or something *more*? I don't know. But I do tend to ever so slightly put my thumb on the scale for a plan of some kind, at least when it comes to my life. And here is the big reason why: I once taught high school seniors, and then I taught college freshmen.

I know that this sounds ridiculous, but truly, I mean this. It is some amazing karma, some ideal circle-of-life perfection, the kind novelists won't write because it seems far too convenient to possibly be true. It's *The Lion King*, only without the lions, puppets, and plot.

You have to understand that when I taught seniors at THSB, we adults tried *so* hard to get them ready for college, but it was a hopeless task. Those students were not into it. They wanted to enjoy their senior year, which had long been promised in American television and film as a glorious time of footloosery. By midwinter, most of them felt their hard work was over—they had gotten into college. Now their lives were set. Besides, didn't they always get As and Bs at THSB? They had no idea what was ahead, and chose to ignore our warnings that college would not be anything like high school, where we teachers were expected to keep them entertained and grade them on a "Hey, you showed up!" scale.

Erica, Danielle, and I worried about this endlessly, knowing that even if we could magically adjust their attitudes (Note: We could not), our students were not ready for college in myriad other ways: financially (even if they managed to land a scholarship, it did not cover personal expenses), geographically (some had barely ever left Brooklyn but were supposed to attend school hundreds of miles away), in terms of the support they got at home (because they were the first to go to college in most of their families, their parents often didn't understand how difficult it was going to be), emotionally, and so on. We couldn't help with much of that, so we tried hard to get them ready academically, at least. But our help was met with eye rolls and scorn.

When many of our students didn't make it through their first semesters at college or passed by the skin of their teeth, we weren't surprised, but we were upset. Yes, our suspicions had been validated, but there was no joy in it, as some of our students lost scholarships, dropped out, returned home, and vowed that college wasn't for them. Others stayed at school, but faced the struggles of their lives thus far to bring up low GPAs while working full-time and juggling family commitments, all in hopes of getting a degree that would set them on a path toward a more stable life. Yet there was little we could do: THSB wasn't really in the college prep business. If anything, we were in the college *admissions* business. After our kids got into college they were on their own, and the demands of the job we had in preparing their former, younger schoolmates meant that there was little time to counsel or support our graduates, even if they asked. It was incredibly frustrating.

———

After four years at THSB, I was beyond ready to move on. In nearly every way, the school was a nightmare: run by a series of increasingly incompetent or corrupt principals, overseen by support administration that was either completely unengaged or in way over their heads, employing a faculty of deeply stressed-out people, and plagued by the same violence and despair that haunted its neighborhood, at least some of the time. The building was dirty and poorly kept, with bedbugs spotted in the hallways. The other schools in the building had little control over their students, who terrorized us. The library was actually falling apart. Laptops kept getting stolen from the laptop cart. I won a prestigious award to develop curriculum with my colleague Kelli, but we had to beg the principal to let us go to the required professional development for it because he had so much trouble getting us subs. We still didn't have bells to change classes. There was no money for new books, so I was still teaching, God help us, *A Separate Peace*, a book so white it makes *Pride and Prejudice* seem like a night at the Apollo. Several of the students smelled so strongly of weed that other kids in the class got sick from the stench. Disciplinary systems changed every year, and the NYCDOE always seemed to have some new initiative to implement, which invariably boiled down to making teachers assume yet another task (like taking on an extra period for small-group counseling). Personally, I was constantly exhausted, tired (once again) of the (slightly shorter but still) long commute, and disgusted with the administration's tacit policy of using any means necessary, up to and including cheating, to get as many of our students as possible to graduate or leave. Worst of all, one of the principals had formed a preposterous but deep-seated grudge against me, which made my life at THSB absolutely miserable.

My close friendship with Erica, Danielle, and a few other teachers at the school, my love for many of our students, and my desire to assure some kind of good future for at least some of them kept me there for longer than I should have stayed. I knew it was time to go two years before I left. Beyond all of the horrors of the school itself, I had no time to write. My writing career was always perpetually perched at the tipping point where, if I just could find the time, I might break through and start making some of my living by it. But I never had the time. There were always lesson plans to write, papers to grade, calls home to make, and incident reports to type up and file, not to mention other jobs to apply for, at other schools.

As I've established, I am not suited for martyrdom, and this was as close as I got. Yet I've come to think of that time as strangely blessed. If God was calling me to be a writer, He had come up with a very clever plan: every effort I made to stay teaching in the NYC-DOE and thus avoid upending my otherwise happy life was churlishly thwarted, while almost every effort I put into writing usually reaped a reward and a way forward. All I needed, I thought, was a year or two to just write. If only I could just catch the break of a little time. So I started putting together applications to several MFA programs. On its merits, it seemed a remarkably stupid plan to leave the reliability of teaching to be a writer, but I decided to try, since writing almost always went well for me, and teaching, increasingly, did not. Besides, honestly, why not? There was no upside to staying at THSB, nowhere else in the NYCDOE seemed to want me, and Stella was gone. Two years to write sounded great to me, so long as I got a scholarship to do it.

Crazily enough, it worked. I got into Pitt. And when I declined their offer because I didn't want to pay for an MFA, they offered me a full ride. So, with fear and trembling, I turned in my notice at THSB. Danielle and Erica and the students who loved me were sad, and I was too. I knew it was unlikely I would ever return to teaching high school again. In fact, I suspected I would never return to full-time teaching again at all, and that seemed okay-ish. As last acts, the administration was cruel to me without cause one more time, using the kindness of the fair warning I gave them that I was leaving against me, and then a couple of the graduating seniors pulled a prank so vile—dumping live worms covered in oil on computer keyboards around the school, including mine—that I, a person who every year has an emotional mid-January parting from my very dead Christmas tree, didn't find it hard to walk out on that last day at all. It was another karmic shove toward Pitt, one strong enough to get me through packing up the apartment I'd lived in for eleven years and saying goodbye to Andrew, to whom I would stay close but no longer see every week.

Before I arrived on campus, I only vaguely grasped that I would be teaching as part of my scholarship package, one class of Seminar in Composition—Pitt's required freshman English class—a term. Pitt keeps those classes small, fewer than twenty students, so they need a lot of people to teach Sem in Comp. That was fine. I knew I could handle it, and I was much more concerned about becoming a student again at thirty-eight and studying writing formally for the first time. For my first few weeks, I almost found teaching relaxing because it was so familiar, although I had to adjust to teaching college students. I learned to be less high-energy and to allow more time for the students—who mostly wanted to be there and certainly were not going to give me the finger as they walked out of the classroom—to just sit and think.

As those weeks turned to months, and I began to know my students, I started to realize that I had been given the perfect karmic reward for all of that worry and grieving back at THSB: I got to help freshmen get used to going to college. Whereas a year before at THSB I had been saying "You guys really do need to start typing your papers before you turn them in, your college professors won't read handwritten work, probably," now I was the college professor at Pitt saying "I won't read a handwritten term paper."

"Y'all, please don't plagiarize; let's learn how to cite correctly" became "I won't read this until you've cited these quotes correctly, unless you want to fail."

"You guys really have to learn to meet your deadlines" became "This is dropped by one letter grade because you've turned it in two days late without explanation."

"Please stop chatting during my short lecture" became . . . well, I didn't need to say anything because one of the young women in my class let the chatting go on for maybe twenty seconds before she shut it down, saying, "I can't even afford to be here, so can you shut up so I can at least learn?" But I have occasionally had to ask a student to stop by my office hours so I can tell them face-to-face that they need to shush, and it's always terrible for them, no matter how low-key I am, because college professors carry much, much more authority than high school teachers.

Is that fair? Not really. But it was a beautiful thing to experience. It was healing too, and suddenly, halfway through my second semester, I realized that I was enjoying teaching. I—get this!— looked forward to going to my classes. I missed the students when I was away from them. And when I was with them, oh boy, did I have a lot to teach them, and a lot to learn from them.

And I finally had enough time to write, and build that career. It felt good. It feels good. One might even say it feels like part of a plan.

If Bruce Springsteen
Wrote about Adjuncts

"Allegheny County Community College Journeyman"

"Hey Mister, Can You Spare a Desk Copy?"

"Incident on I-95 (I Will Be Late for Class)"

"I Can't Remember Your Name, Girl in the Second Row (Wendy?)"

"I'm Gonna Get Fired"

"Second Semester Corporate Buyout"

"From Little Mistakes, Failing Grades Come"

"Columbus Day, My Living Room (Thirty Papers to Grade)"

"Adam Earned a C-"

"Because the Night Belongs to Lesson Plans"

"Blinded by the SMART Board Projector"

"You Can Glance Around (but You'd Better Not Cheat)"

"Workin' on the Curricula"

"It's So Hard to Stay Awake in the Fourth Class of the Day"

"Land of Scope and Themes"

"If I Should Fall Behind (My Sub Plans Are in My Mailbox)"

"Darkness on the Edge of Campus Where the Adjuncts Have to Park"

On Adjuncting

Working as an adjunct professor is a difficult job: underpaid and overworked, most adjuncts go without benefits, drive hundreds of miles every week to teach at several campuses, do not get paid over the summer, and rely on other jobs or even governmental assistance to make ends meet. But many of them love teaching their subject and hope to become full-time professors, so they put up with the indignities and unfairness of the job, knowing that they earn 75 percent less than the tenured professor down the hall teaching the same course. The adjunct life is about as different from the stereotypical image of a professor as you can get, which makes the job somehow worse: it's one thing to work super hard all the time, but quite another to work super hard while most people around you assume that 1) you're not working hard at all and 2) you make six figures for not working hard.

I should know: after I finished my MFA in Creative Writing at Pitt, I worked as an adjunct there and at a couple of other schools in Western Pennsylvania. It was a grim time in my life. My father had passed away after a short illness, and like my mother, brother, sister-in-law, and aunts, I was in mourning, weeping on the hours-long commutes to and from various universities. Still, I was glad to have the work, which was just enough to live on when combined with the money I was beginning to pull in as a writer. I was especially glad to continue to teach at Pitt, which was home to me, and where I, like all adjuncts there, could buy into the benefits package and keep the same insurance I had as a student. But mostly I was sad and weary, extremely doubtful about whether I could keep teaching as a career.

Eventually things worked out for me, and I landed a full-time, if temporary, professorial job as a visiting lecturer in the English department at Pitt, and then, wonder of wonders, became a lecturer there. Which is why I'd like to write less about my experience as an adjunct and more about what it must have been like to have been one of my students. After all, individual professors come and go, but the trend toward hiring more and more adjuncts instead of tenured and/or full-time faculty affects millions of American college students, who deserve better and are almost always paying for it.

Take my student Andrea. She's hypothetical but based on a student I knew when I taught at a small university in southwestern Pennsylvania, which I'll call the University of Pagford. Andrea was a good student, not at the top of her class but engaged and learning. She asked to meet with me to discuss the essay she'd written for my freshman composition class, something roughly half of all my freshman students will ask to do at some point. Her essay grade was a B, and Andrea wanted to know why,* not to mention how to improve it.

Let's also stipulate, for the sake of clarity, that Andrea was a pleasant young woman who wasn't just trying to haggle me up to a B+; nope, she was a thoughtful writer with real potential. In short, Andrea was the type of student any decent teacher would enjoy

---

* I tried to keep myself fairly footnote-free in this book, although I love them. But here I have to point out the titular reference that expands the title's meaning!

spending a half hour of intense revision work with, and since I am a decent-ish teacher, I was in.

If Andrea was able to stop by my office hours at Pagford, great! No problem. We'd meet, she'd revise, her grade would go up as would her comprehension. Yay, learning!

Oh, wait—actually, there was a bit of a problem: My office hours were also my lunch hours. So my choices were: eat in front of Andrea, which she understandably might have found rude; skip lunch (ahem: I have never in my life skipped lunch); or try to eat quickly in the ten minutes between the end of my class and her arrival.

The last was probably the best option, and the one I usually chose, but there was another issue. My "office" at Pagford was a desk that I shared with another adjunct in a small room. The "adjuncts' office" had five full-sized desks packed into it, two edge to edge by the door, the other three squeezed in together against the other wall. Ten of us were supposed to split them, two per desk with a drawer for each. Two of those desks, including the one I shared, were in use during the hour before my lunch/office hours, which made sneaking in early to eat tricky.

There was another problem with this setup. Because of the two always-present-during-lunch-hour adjuncts, there wasn't any way to have privacy in there with Andrea, particularly unfortunate because her essay was about her obsessive-compulsive disorder. In it, she revealed that she'd never told anyone outside of her family and girlfriend about her condition before, so I really didn't want to force her to talk about it in front of two strangers (and possibly their visiting students).

But even if Andrea had written about her pet rabbit Floopy, the other two professors probably wanted to continue to sit at their desks, so there would have been—and I mean this quite literally—no room for Andrea and me to sit together in the office. I couldn't actually sit at my desk when one of the colleagues who worked at the desk across from me was there: there was only enough aisle room for one of us at a time. That was why I almost always put a note up as to where I'd be and took my sandwich to the campus library nearby to sneakily eat my lunch in a deserted corner during my office hours. But Andrea and I could not meet in the library! You have to be quiet in the library! (As I learned once when two students near me were thoroughly shushed from quietly discussing their homework. Also, I can't discuss anything quietly, but I'm willing to grant that as an exception unique to me.)

Luckily, there was a solution for Andrea and me, thanks to a quirk of scheduling. We could meet in our classroom, which I happened to have for both my 11 A.M. and 1 P.M. classes that particular semester. That was great, buuuut it was a classroom in use by many other professors and classes on that busy campus during the course of the week. Thus, I could never leave anything there, so I wasn't able to consult any of my many helpful books on writing or loan one to Andrea, the kind of thing my professors did for me. I *could* have left books at my office desk, but I would have had to interrupt the other two adjuncts and their students to get them during Andrea's visit.

But at least this classroom fix was better than what Andreas at another school where I was adjuncting had to put up with. There, I didn't have an office, not even half a desk in an overstuffed room, and the room where my class met was used by another class during my "office" hours, so I usually met with students in the hallway, sitting on the floor, or, if it was nice out, on a bench outside. Once on a rainy day, desperate, I met with a female student in the foyer to the women's room.

Anyway, back to Andrea. We got the classroom and it wasn't ideal but okay. We discussed her essay, I taught my afternoon class, and I ate the other half of my lunch in my car on the way to my next class. We did it! Yay, learning! I was a helpful professor to my student.

But what if Andrea couldn't make my specific office hours? Maybe she was in the drama club, which rehearsed at noon. Or she had to meet with a professor in a class she was failing. Or she might have had a job that began at one o'clock, or a kid to pick up from day care at a quarter to one, or she might have needed to give her mom a ride to work no later than twelve thirty. These are all reasonable explanations of why she couldn't meet during my office hours, and so we might have had to find another time.

Andrea might have proposed that we meet before class, at 9:45 A.M., which in theory would have been fine, except that I commuted ninety minutes via the Pennsylvania Turnpike. What I learned during my first few weeks of commuting was that the turnpike, which I'd previously always seen as a boring means to a more exciting end, was actually a *Mad Max*–esque staging ground for the kind of car accidents that occur when truck and car drivers jockey for the left lane. My commute slowed to a crawl (or had to be detoured) at least once a week. Thus, although I gave myself two hours to make the trip, it was harder to be more accurate than "there in time for class," and I hated to make Andrea play that roulette wheel with me.

Also, no one ever explained to me how to get a faculty parking pass so I parked off-campus, about a ten-minute walk away.

Also, sometimes the professor who had a 9 A.M. class in our classroom didn't leave until 9:57, and sometimes the building staff didn't unlock the adjunct office until after ten, so we'd have to meet in the hall anyway.

Okay, Andrea might have asked, clearly a little frustrated, could she come by after my 1 P.M. class was done and talk to me then? Yes! I would have said. Sort of! I could meet as long as it was on Fridays, but alas, on Mondays and Wednesdays I had to leave the classroom no later than 2:20 P.M. (factoring in that ten-minute walk) to get to Pitt to teach that evening. Remember it was eighty minutes away— if there weren't any accidents—and I had to eat dinner too and get there in time for my office hours with my Pitt Andreas, which had to be before our 6 P.M. class because no one wanted to meet at 8:30 P.M., even if I was fine with it.

Whew, okay. So that brings us back to lunchtime, which was when Andrea said she couldn't meet. But perhaps she turned out to be both determined and accommodating and declared that she would tell her boss or her mom or her babysitter she was going to be fifteen minutes late on Wednesday, and that she'd bring her lunch with her, and thus we ate lunch together as we sat in the classroom and talked about her paper. That's awesome. I mean, yay, learning, and more specifically, yay, Andrea!

But most students are not Andrea and, frankly, they shouldn't have to be as superhumanly dedicated as her in order to have a fifteen-minute conference with their Comp 101 professor. I'm not Bono, for God's sake. I shouldn't be harder to schedule time with than the pope.

Clearly, my being an adjunct was not good for my students. And while I'd love to think that my pure wonderfulness as a teacher made up for my adjunct status, I'm not sure it did. I mean, it was all just random luck for Andrea. If she had just happened to register for a different section of the course, she might have had a full-time professor, who might have been able to meet with her at nine forty-five, or two thirty, or five, in an office with a door that could close or nearly close, and with a stack of books that could be lent out. Andrea could have sat in a comfortable chair, perhaps with a cup of tea, to discuss her extremely personal paper that she wanted to improve. She might have had time to really talk through what was troubling her about the paper, and even bring back a new draft after working on it overnight. If Andrea was struggling with her mental illness, or her finances, or even with grammar, the full-time professor had the time to offer initial care, and would have known about people she could speak to on campus or resources she could investigate there.

It gets worse: if Andrea turned out to be talented, that full-time professor could encourage Andrea to consider English as a major. She also might suggest course sequencing and which professors Andrea should seek out. The full-time professor would have access to university letterhead to write Andrea a permission letter to register for a class she really wanted to take outside of her sequence. She would know the school policies about such things. She could recommend a scholarship fund to apply to, an internship to consider, or an on-campus writing group to join. She could cheer for Andrea at graduation and other senior-year events, because she wouldn't be at her third job. Should they really form a bond, that professor's email address would presumably stay the same so Andrea could email her for years to come, whereas my email got deactivated two weeks after I left Pagford.

Instead, Andrea got me. She paid the same for her credits whether she had the professor with the office, tea, and chair, or me. That's not fair. And while Andrea was specifically my student, this is not a specifically English department problem. Science adjuncts can't get into labs to work with their students there. Math adjuncts don't have early access to classrooms to write out equations beforehand. Foreign-language adjuncts don't have borrowing privileges at campus libraries and thus can't take out the needed books. The long hours, the long commute, the lack of materials, the sharing of space, these are all problems that most adjuncts have, and none of us can always avoid passing them on to our own Andreas.

Look, I know most students aren't Andreas. But every student deserves the chance to become an Andrea in college, and professors are supposed to give them that chance. Because I was an adjunct, I couldn't.

I had a note on my To Do list every week that semester: "Talk to Andrea about switching to English as a major." I never crossed it off, because I never remembered to do it until I was already in the car, twenty miles down the road, off to the next class.

Classic College Movies Updated for the Adjunct Era

Who's Afraid of Virginia Woolf?

Martha, the alcoholic daughter of the dean, is married to George, an adjunct professor. She invites Nick, another adjunct professor, and his wife over for a drink. But Nick has way too many papers to grade, and George can't spare a minute away from his academic job search to socialize anyway. A drunk Martha falls asleep on the couch as the credits roll.

Run Time: 5 minutes

The Paper Chase

On his first day at Harvard Law School, James Hart assumes that his professor, Charles W. Kingsfield Jr., will begin the class by going over the syllabus. Instead, Professor Kingsfield asks him a challenging question.

"I don't know," answers Hart. "I totally can't believe you asked me a difficult question in front of my peers. You should've respected that I'm an introvert."

"Oh my God, I'm so sorry," replies Kingsfield. "Listen, don't put this on my end-of-term evaluation, okay? I really need this job. I'll give you an A for today. No! Hey, everyone in the class gets an A too, okay?"

Run Time: 17 minutes

Good Will Hunting

MIT professor Gerald Lambeau is impressed by the intellect of Will Hunting, a janitor who solved an extremely difficult math problem, but Will needs help processing his complex emotions and anger. Lambeau turns to his estranged former college roommate, Dr. Sean Maguire, for help. Sadly, Maguire, an adjunct professor who must shuttle between three campuses in two states and teach seven classes a semester to stay off the dole, can't find a minute to call Lambeau back. Will ends up in jail by the age of twenty-three, Lambeau never goes out on a limb for another student, and Maguire is fired for being late to class because of a car pileup on I-90.

Run Time: 1 hour

Legally Blonde

In pursuit of her ex, Elle Woods arrives at Harvard to attend law school, but doesn't fit in. To make things worse, she is quickly kicked out of class by a tenured professor. Crying, Elle flees, only to run into Emmett, a handsome, young adjunct professor.

"Do you have any words of comfort for me, Professor?" Elle asks plaintively.

"God, I wish," Emmett calls over his shoulder as he races to the parking lot. "But I'm on my way to my other teaching job at the Worcester Polytechnic Institute!"

Elle goes back to her dorm, packs her bags, and returns to California, where she marries her father's business partner's younger son, a loveless union that ends in divorce after two years.

Run Time: 45 minutes

A Beautiful Mind

In lieu of a tenured position, John Nash is offered an adjunct teaching post at Princeton. "Take it!" the Paul Bettany character only he can see says. "You can live handsomely on three thousand dollars a semester! Let's buy a silver tea service!" Nash ends up homeless in Newark, and never wins a Nobel Prize, obvs.

Run Time: 15 minutes

Mona Lisa Smile

Katherine Ann Watson is hired as an adjunct professor at Oakland State University. On her first day of class, she realizes that her anxious students have already memorized the textbook and her syllabus.

"Oh, that's great," she says. "At least this class is going to go smoothly!"

Just then, the president of the college enters and says, "Professor Watson, I've had to give this class to a tenured teacher who's so terrible no one signed up for his regular course."

"I'm fired?" Watson replies.

"Oh, no! You can't be fired if you're a contractual employee! No, no, you've just been *let go.*"

Katherine departs Oakland State forever.

Run Time: 10 minutes

Pitch Perfect 2

On their way home from winning yet another a cappella competition, the Bellas see Beca Mitchell's father sitting alone with a large stack of papers in the lobby of a building on Barden University's campus.

"What's your stupid father doing?" Fat Amy asks Beca.

"Oh, he doesn't have an office and he's teaching four classes a day, so probably, like, grading?" Beca replies.

The Bellas look aghast: There are professors? Who work hard?

"We're going to help your father, and all adjunct professors!" Fat Amy declares.

The Bellas disband to become an activist student protest group, demanding better conditions for all the adjuncts at Barden. Their movement spreads throughout the United States, as one collegiate a cappella group after another abandons their renditions of "Under Pressure" and "Carol of the Bells" to actually change their campuses and the country.

Run Time: 3 hours

A Brief List of What Students Have Called Me

Shannon.

Miss Shannon.

Ms. Shannon.

Mythhannon. (Many preschoolers' attempt at "Ms. Shannon.")

Miss Reed.

Ms. Reed.

Dr. Reed. (Not a doctor! Despite being specifically ruled out on my syllabi, someone invariably will stick with this all semester.)

Professor Reed.

P. Reed.

Mrs. Reed. (No.)

Sharon Reed. (NO!)

Ms. Shannon Screed. (I think this was a typo, not a judgment.)

Ma'am. (Ouch.)

Madame. (I'm into it.)

Miss. (One of my colleagues at THSB promised the entire class As if they could keep from calling her "Miss" for an entire week. They didn't last even one class.)

Literally any of my colleagues' names, including male colleagues
who were twenty years older than me.

Mama Reed.

"Mom? OH MY GOD I mean, NOT MOM."

Lady.

The Lady Reed. (One of my favorites.)

GURL. (Also one of my favorites.)

Bitch.

Basic bitch.

Wishes she was a basic bitch. (Note: I do not.)

Slave owner. (A THSB student's response to my asking her to be
quiet backstage during a performance.)

My heroin. (I think/hope they meant "heroine.")

Wonder Woman.

The nicest person in the world.

The meanest professor on campus. (These last two by the same student, a week apart.)

A fat hoe.

The best.

On Student Evaluations

Author's note: Because I can't ask permission to quote them directly, all quotes in this essay paraphrase actual student comments on evaluations.

Pitt asks students to evaluate their professors and their courses during the last month of each semester, before grading begins. Those results, mysteriously called the OMETs for reasons no one could explain to me, are then compiled and emailed to professors well after the semester is over. By then, our students have left for holiday or summer adventures, and the campus is quiet. When I take books back to the libraries on campus, it looks so deserted that I half expect to see whatever is the Pittsburghian equivalent of tumbleweeds roll by.

But the semester is not settled for me. I'm still thinking about what worked and what went badly in class, ruing the mistakes I made, and feeling some small measure of joy about what we accomplished. My brain hasn't let go of the students I worked with yet. I'm still in constant conversation with myself about what I might do to reach or help them, only to repeatedly realize with a start that they are gone.

So when the OMETs arrive, I'm not in Margaritaville. Reading their evaluations of me, completed during what are often the most stressful weeks of their semester, feels like a call to further communication. I want to email each commenter and discuss their thoughts. Their praise makes me want to cry tears of happy gratitude for our mutual growth. Their critique makes me surly with aggrieved anger: "I *tried*," I want to scream. I was not perfect, but there is no perfection!

But that would be very unprofessional, and also there's no one to scream at, or explain to, or try to connect with. They're gone. The semester is over. And the evaluations are anonymous, anyway.

———

At least I'm not alone when it's OMETs time. Many of my colleagues post about them on social media. We tell each other that we don't have to read them right away. In fact, we don't have to read them at all, really. Only those of us who have jobs we have to reapply for need to interact with them in order to copy and paste the responses into our applications, and I have mastered the ability to let my vision go blurry while I do this.

Eh, who are we kidding? We all read them immediately anyway.

My female-identifying colleagues and I enjoy sharing the most outlandish things our male-identifying students wrote about us. Not a semester goes by without an eighteen-year-old male student explaining to us how we might do our jobs better, often suggesting we do something ludicrous ("Get rid of grades!") or not allowed by the university ("We should only meet every other week."). My favorite comment along these lines was "Hey, ease up on the feminism!" I did not mention the word "feminism" at any point in that class, but I did assign readings from a list of writers that was 75 percent female. My very being must have been an argument for feminism, which, frankly, is one of the nicest things a student has ever implied about me.

This group share is sort of depressing, but I think it helps us to see that each of us deals with this type of respondent: those stu-

dents who fail to understand that while we will read their comments with great interest, no one else will, and that they might
have more effectively given us their critique in person.

———

I prioritize clarity in my classroom, and I'm funny. I've convinced
myself that this is why my evaluations are almost always very good.
I often read feedback like "This class was the high point of my week"
and "Thank you for keeping the mood bright." As I make a real effort
not to bring my fatigue and ill temper into the classroom, I appreciate that this is noticed. I recognize that after a while it's expected,
but I also know that I enjoy class more when I make the effort too.

But not everyone likes funny. There is always one comment
from one student in every class along the lines of "The classroom
is no place for humor" or "Writing is very serious to me, and I don't
like to be in a room with so much laughing." This makes me sad for
the person who wrote it. It also makes me feel like a flibbertigibbet
of a girl, one who doesn't belong in the hallowed halls of academia.

———

Despite the anonymity of the OMETs, I can usually tell who wrote
what, especially when they write at length. I try to warn the students about this. I tell the class that everyone has a distinctive writing style, and that after a semester or more of reading their work
closely, I recognize each of them in their words. "If being anonymous is important to you," I say, "you may want to deliberately disguise yourself and your writing on the OMETs."

Most students don't care if I know who wrote what. Some probably should, though; once, a young woman in my class wrote several
paragraphs on the OMETs about an incident when she felt I had ignored her when we happened to be on the same bus. I hadn't heard

her greeting, but when she confronted me angrily about my slight at the time, I apologized profusely. From her comments on the OMETs, it was clear that she didn't believe or accept my apology. She had smiled at me and been cheerful throughout the semester, though.

———

A student stays to talk with me after class. She wants to explain why she won't be able to attend our last session. She's really bummed about it, but the professor of the class she's in before mine has decided to give them their final during their last class, so it will run over into our meeting time. He's going to Venice for the summer, she says, so he says he needs the extra time to grade before he leaves.

This isn't allowed, I, who am not going to Venice for the summer, tell her. The university rules state that professors have to give finals (or have final projects and portfolios due) during finals week, specifically to avoid this kind of "starting the summer early" by professors. She says she's very stressed-out about having to study for a test that's now eight days earlier than she was expecting, and happening during a week when classes meet regularly and much work is due. Also, the professor said he would make the final easier because of the rushed schedule. She doesn't like that either, and he gives her the creeps so she doesn't want to talk to him.

I say, "Well, you can report this to the chair of his department." She looks uneasy. "Or," I suggest, "put that on his OMETs." She immediately looks relieved, glad that there's something she can do.

———

Studies on student evaluations consistently find that students rate professors who've given them good grades higher than those in whose classes they've earned lower grades, regardless of how much they feel they've learned. In my classes, students can redo work as often as they like to get the grade they desire, an idea I adapted from my mentors in the English department. Not that many students actually revise all that often, but those who really want to—whether because of an inner drive to learn as much as they can about writing, a disturbingly persistent perfectionism, or just a desire to get an A—like that they can. More to the point, the entire class seems to really appreciate this policy, even those who make no use of it, because they sense it turns at least some of the power of grading over to them. I really like this policy too. I find it so much easier to write "C" on a paper when I know the student has a chance to revise it up to an A.

I didn't realize that this policy likely boosts my OMET scores, but I'm pleased to learn from those studies that it probably does. Maybe I should stop saying I get good evaluations because I'm funny. Maybe I know what I'm doing. This is a good policy I've stumbled into, helpful to all of us and promoting learning.

———

I started talking to my students about the OMETs after my first year of teaching at Pitt, and continue to do so to this day. I do not tell them what to write. I encourage them to fill them out for all their professors, emphasizing that we do read them and keep them in mind, which I know is true for my department, at least.

I tell them that if they have a real concern, they should email me directly so I can work it out with them before the end of the semester, as OMETs are due before grades go out. I tell them what I've told you: it drives me nuts to find out that there was a problem long after I could do anything about it. I also tell them that the OMETs are where they can put their concerns down safely if they just don't feel that they can talk to me or another professor directly.

I try to explain how they have power over me too, via the

OMETs, which are a real factor in why I moved from adjunct to full time, and then to a permanent job at Pitt. They contain a double power, I explain: a communication to me, and a communication to my bosses.

I also talk about the different job titles at Pitt, and how, even though they know all of the faculty as "professor," there are differences in salaries, responsibilities, and duties across the categories. This involves explaining the difference between tenured professors, which they always think we all are, and non-tenure-stream professors, which is what almost all of us actually are. My students are often startled to learn that full-time, tenure-track professors teach fewer classes than those not on the tenure track, and I'm startled too, every time, to know that people who make a lot more than me teach two classes a semester, while I teach three. When I was an adjunct, I told them I was an adjunct, and what that meant. Now that I'm full-time, I tell them that I am. I show them where they can find this information for all their professors.

When I first started talking about this, as an adjunct, my anxiety/desperation about my career path must have shown, because some of the comments I read later were along the lines of "YOU SHOULD HIRE SHANNON AS A REAL PROFESSOR! You're FOOLS if you don't! She's all that's right and good in the world!!!" I've tried harder not to recruit my students to the cause of me since then. I force myself to be offhand about it, as though I have my pick of jobs awaiting me should my contract not be extended.

———

One student complained at some length on the OMETs that I was hearing-impaired. He found it problematic that I asked him to repeat himself at times. "Professors can be disabled, but not like that," he evaluated.

———

The section of the OMETs I most resent are the "suggestions for improving the course" responses. The only response that makes me smile—and one that I get every class and every semester—is "Nothing, this course is great, thank you, Shannon!" It's not that I think the class was flawless, but I appreciate that the student saw that I tried my best and it was good enough.

But to be fair, even students who loved the class see possibilities for it that I do not, which is the point of the question. I tell myself to stop being a whiner, so I grit my teeth and read their notes. At the end, while I dismiss the ridiculous ones ("We should read less" and "I think you should meet with each of us individually for a half hour once a week" and "You should wear red more often"), I do take others. One person suggested I make my email subject lines better than the university's default ("From the Desk of Shannon Reed"), which I groaned over, but which was . . . a good idea. My students often comment on how they appreciate knowing what the email is about before opening it. I am inordinately proud of myself for taking this suggestion, and always tell my students I did.

———

An evaluation that truly shocked me was from a student who declared that I hated books and had spent the entire semester "sneering" at them. He accused me of having a secret agenda to lure the class away from reading. He said I'd ruined reading for him. Reading this felt like being slapped.

He also said that my critique of his writing was meritless, and he knew this because I had no bylines to brag about. He looked for me on the internet, he said, and except for a few "piddling publications" I barely existed as a professional writer, and thus shouldn't be critiquing students at all. Yet, he said, I buttonholed my students into listening to me "pontificate for most of the class" about my own nonexistent accomplishments.

Ow. That hurt. But I then reread his comments and had to laugh. He'd completely overshot the mark. It would have been much more effective to stick closer to the truth—not that I hate books (no one who's ever even just seen me could believe that) but that perhaps I'm a snob about books. More effective too, to have said that for a writer with my credits, I'm not a good critic, instead of apparently trying to convince the reader of my OMETs that the *New Yorker* and the *Washington Post* are piddling. He should have taken me down for being too chatty and flighty, perhaps, but not for being a braggart. I'm full of flaws, but not the ones he made up.

After reading it again, I told myself that he didn't understand that I would see it and that he also didn't realize that the people who will read it as part of my job application for another year at Pitt have known me for years as their student and now as their colleague. They wouldn't believe this.

I decided I didn't believe it either.

I could tell right away who this student was. He had a very distinctive writing style, as "piddling" might indicate. A few months later, I was in charge of a literary journal to which he submitted an essay he hadn't liked my critique about. He hadn't revised it. I sent it to the editor without comment, grateful I wasn't responsible for choosing the works that made it in. But I was neither surprised nor displeased when I saw his essay wasn't chosen. Does it count as a lesson about the importance of kindness and the smallness of any literary world if the student doesn't know he's been taught it?

———

A few months after those OMETs, the student who felt I slighted her on the bus asked me to write a letter of recommendation for her. I gently declined. I didn't know she disliked me that much until I read the OMETs, but now I couldn't shake what she wrote. I would have written her a good recommendation.

———

A few semesters ago, one of my student evaluators wrote, "When I grow up, I want to be Shannon" on my OMETs. My heart sang upon reading that. At my lowest points, when the basement has flooded and my mortgage has skyrocketed, when I wonder if I should continue teaching or find just about any other career for better pay, when I think about the male professors who work much less hard but make far more money than me and my female-identifying colleagues, when I can't afford the fancy cheese and I feel a little too emotional about it, I remember that she took the time to write that, knowing I would read it. Then my evaluation of my job still stands: there's none better in the world.

My Ideal Student Evaluation Questionnaire

1. Of the five amazing books we read this semester, which do you think you are most likely to quote from memory, tagging me, on your Instagram page?
2. Please tell me about the moment when you realized that despite all your complaints about this class, it actually had changed your life.
3. Tell me a couple of things the other professors do that are annoying, like, nothing big, but just enough that I can feel ever so faintly superior to them in faculty meetings.
4. If I ever write a movie based on your class, who do you want to play you? What about me? What about that kid who was on his phone through every class and then dropped out after he said Shakespeare wrote *The Scarlet Letter*?
5. Do you remember that one day I did something different with my hair? Did it work? No? Any suggestions for improvement? Can you recommend a hairstyling product that only the youths know about?

6. What else was going on with you besides taking this class? What were your triumphs and struggles this semester? I have very little insight about your life, so fill me in.

7. I'd really love to have a cool nickname, the way my high school students used to call me Mama Reed. That was ironic because I was so young, but wouldn't work at all now because I am aged. Suggestions?

8. What did you learn in this class that had nothing to do with me?

9. Did I do anything that was clearly not meant to offend or wound but did so anyway? Can you tell me, but, like, in a really, really nice way? I'd like to make it right, but I'm sensitive.

10. Will you email me this summer, once in a while, maybe after you read a book you think I should read?

11. Oh! I have a selfie from the day I tried that hair thing, let me know if you want to see it.

12. Wasn't that last monologue in *Lincoln in the Bardo* amazing? Do you think any of us will ever write anything that good? (Yeah, I think so too. I mean, maybe not you, maybe not me, but one of us. Someday!)

13. Wait, before we wrap up, did you see Richard Linklater's *Boyhood*? Do you think it in any way lives up to the hype? I just did not get it.

14. Not really a question, but just a gentle reminder to thank me if you win a National Book Award. Remember, it's "Shannon" not "Sharon."

Worst, Weirdest, and Best

'm asked at least once a week what it's like to be a professional writer. My usual response of "It's good but hard!" is often not deemed sufficient by the askers. No, they want the *details*. What time do I get up? Do I use a laptop? How do I keep myself motivated? Are there any particular shoes I recommend to other people who want to go pro? (Now that you mention it, thanks to my recent sponsorship deal with Adidas, I'm pleased to recommend their WRT 24/7 model!)

No one ever asks me these kinds of questions about teaching. In fact, no one ever asks me anything about teaching at all, except for extremely specific advice about whether they should take a job in the NYCDOE (No, I tell them, you should not.). This lack of interest makes a certain kind of sense. Writers seem exotic and rare while almost all of us have been around teachers at work for a significant chunk of our lives. We feel, and this is not a stretch, that we know what teaching entails.

Fair enough. But I do wish I had the chance to talk about what it's like to be a teacher more often. There are so many questions I wish I got to answer, from what's my favorite part of being a teacher (the students) to what's my least favorite part of being a teacher (chasing down homework, which somehow I am still doing even though I teach adults now). I wish people asked me what my favorite book to teach is (*Life After Life* by Kate Atkinson) and which one I was sorry I had picked (sadly, also *Life After Life* by Kate Atkinson— one of my classes was really not having it). And I wish they asked me what the worst, weirdest, and best things about teaching are, because I have those answers on the tip of my tongue. Actually, I'm just going to pretend that you asked me what those are. How nice, thank you!

Since you asked, I can say that, to me, the worst thing about being a teacher is the tyranny of the clock. Now, I appreciate a well-kept schedule. I consider arriving to a movie less than fifteen minutes beforehand to be slightly late, and I get snippy if I realize I'm going to arrive at the dentist on time instead of a half hour early. But in teaching, the relentlessness of the schedule really gets to me. There's no room to change or modify the ceaseless passage of regimented time blocks. No matter how good the discussion is during third period, the bell will ring and we'll move on. And even if it's clear that the best thing would be for fifth period to end ten minutes early, we can't. Since it's all interconnected, my keeping third period for ten minutes or letting fifth period out early would mess up every other teacher's life (as was made very clear to me when a certain teacher at THSB let her second period wander down the hall to become my very early third period at least twice a week). I hate that.

It's a little better teaching at the college level, where no one much cares if we start a bit late or end early, although Pitt's so busy that another class will want our classroom if we run long. I particularly love teaching night classes, where my students are a little bit slower to race out of the room since their classes are done for the day. But I still long to not spend a significant portion of my adult life anticipating the exact moment when I have to be on my way or

I'll be late. Let me finish watching this show, or write until I'm out of things to say, or actually have time to make all the copies before 6 P.M. Just ease up on the schedule once in a while. In my summers, I get deep joy out of not living my life on a school schedule.

The weirdest thing about teaching for me is easy to pinpoint. I've gotten used to it by now, but for the first few years of teaching high school it completely freaked me out to realize that every student in the room was, at least in theory, staring at me. This was particularly fraught at Stella, since I was the only person in the room not in uniform, the default peacock among the sparrows, no matter what I was wearing. But even now, the sudden realization that my students can stare/are staring at my butt, back, hairstyle, elbows, whatever, can throw me. It's odd to be analyzed like that. No one ever talked to me about the on-public-display aspect of teaching before I started. I was better prepared than most, I suspect, because of my theatre background. But I think it's warped more than a few teachers. It is so strange, especially in a culture that dislikes aging and finds the signs of it to be distasteful, to have so many youths staring at us old crones.

On the flip side, though, I do like that I have always felt justified in dressing well because I was always completely sure someone would notice.

The best part about teaching? I know I'm supposed to say the students, but I already said they're my *favorite* part of teaching, so let me stipulate, yes, of course, my students are wonderful. They light up my life. They make me whole.

That said, I think the best part about teaching is the academic year. Not just the summers. I mean, I like the summers. Pitt has a four-ish-month summer, which is swell. But no, the whole year. The rise and fall of the seasons. How we show up in August or September, full of tales of wonderful or awful summers that somehow dissipate when we try to say them aloud. That first fall day when everyone wears a sweater. That second fall day when everyone again wears a sweater because now they actually need to wear a sweater, it's not just anticipatory. Autumn fogs out our classroom windows. Celebrating Halloween with the twin traditions of throwing bags of candy to the class and being careful not to make fun of that one student who alone wore a full costume. The counting down toward fall break, then Thanksgiving, then the holiday break. Finals week, or as I like to call it, Early Holiday Break for Professors. Everyone coming back in their new winter clothes, typing on their new laptops. The long, dark days of winter, and complaining to each other about them. Valentine's Day and the drama that inevitably arises from it. The beginning of spring. Then, because I teach in Pittsburgh, the harsh return of winter. And the continuation of that harsh return. And then, finally, at last, spring, and finals, and freedom. I love it.

When I worked in an office for a couple of years, it was very nice in a number of notable ways, most specifically that I never had any work to take home with me, which was magical. But I missed the seasons. We were never working toward anything—no finals, no breaks. Just a relentless corporate slog to perhaps getting promoted or whatever, something, someday. That I did not like. I missed my academic year. When Labor Day weekend rolled around the second year of my office job, I was like a dog sniffing the air for a familiar scent: What was that? Why were my nerves jangling? Why did I feel anticipatory yet sort of morose? It wasn't until I got back to teaching and felt that way every Labor Day weekend since that I realized the academic calendar was in my body, and I would never break free from it. Nor do I want to.

There you have it: worst, weirdest, and best parts about teaching for me. I bet if you ask another teacher, they'll give you completely different answers. And I'd bet they'd love it if you asked.

A Short Essay by a Student Who Googled the Professor Instead of Reading *Jane Eyre*

Reading *Jane Eyre* reminds me of something Benedict Cumberbatch once said: "I am a feminist, too." I learned of Mr. Cumberbatch's feelings when I happened upon an Instagram feed that might be familiar to readers of this essay, where I saw it covered with several panting tongue and eggplant emojis. I'd like to dedicate this, my paper on *Jane Eyre*, to him, and to all men who, like me, are also feminists, and also to all women, who are, of course, the best. I am pro-women, and I am pro-freedom of speech, even to the point of defending the right of professors to publicly post to their Instagram accounts, possibly without realizing that said accounts could be easily found.

Women are the most important characters in *Jane Eyre*. They do all the things that are done and none of the things that are not done in the novel. In terms of themes, which I've been asked to write about here, I'd like to point to the well-known parts of the novel where Jane faces major complications in her life and must decide what to do.

This reminds me of Jane's first words to the reader, "There was no possibility of taking a walk that day." From there, it is clear that the main character will decide many things, starting with deciding not to take a walk. The decisions she makes will influence the course of her life.

It all makes for a fascinating journey, much like that of Hermione in the Harry Potter books, who is the most important of the less-important characters in those books. She, too, is a woman, which is no coincidence. If you are wondering why I bring up Hermione who is not in *Jane Eyre* (unless there is another character named Hermione in there), the answer is that I got to thinking about her because of a post I saw on Instagram. In the Instagram post, a woman I know was wearing a T-shirt that read "Hermione Was the Real Chosen One" and hoisting a very large stein of beer.

I am so glad *Jane Eyre* was assigned to me. I think I learned a lot from reading it and will think differently about women named Jane who do or do not go walking from now on, and all the decisions women have to make. And just in case that does not seem like a complex enough theme to draw from *Jane Eyre*, I would just mention that not everything I read in college can be as interesting as the series of photos I'll call the Naughty Witches Series, which I found many thumb-scrolls toward the bottom of that same Instagram account. This is the end of my essay on *Jane Eyre*.

Moral Quandaries for Professors

1. You see a runaway trolley approaching at high speed, destined to plow into five books lying on the track. These books are by the colleague who was recently chosen for a promotion over you. You can pull a lever that would cause the trolley to cross over to an entirely empty track.

   The quandary: Which of Panera's salads are you going to order for lunch?

2. A lifeboat full of your students is on the ocean, and a terrifying storm approaches. Either some of the students will need to sacrifice themselves for the survival of the others, or the entire boat will capsize and all will likely drown.

   The quandary: Should you accept late work from the students who make it, even if they don't have a doctor's note?

3. The university library emails. They are winnowing the stacks as part of an annual downsizing, and intend to discard all books not checked out in the last year.

   The quandary: Is it okay to interrupt your TA's afternoon class to send her over to the library to check out all your books, or should you wait until she's dismissed?

4. Many students skip the last day of class, believing that little happens then. Even an absence policy does not prevent this, as they simply save their absences for that day. This greatly annoys you, so you start bringing homemade baked goods on the last day of the semester to entice them to attend. A student in the class who will fail if he misses class one more time has mentioned that he is allergic to peanuts. He has also repeatedly asked you to read his "manifesto" about *Star Trek*.

   The quandary: Do you tell him that you're making peanut butter cookies or not?

5. You are out for a stroll around the reservoir one day and notice that a child is apparently drowning. You dive in and manage to save him. A passerby takes a photo of you rescuing the child.

   The quandary: Do you send the photo to your own alumni magazine or to the media relations office of the university where you currently teach, or both?

6. A friend applies for an open teaching position in your department. He is likely not the most qualified person to apply, but you have been friends for a very long time.

   The quandary: Do you offer to marry your friend in order to invoke spousal privilege for job placement?

7. After swearing you to secrecy, a higher-ranking colleague confesses that he has been having an affair with a student. You beg him to tell the chair of your program about the affair, but he refuses, reminding you that you have sworn to keep silent.

   The quandary: Do you call the chair immediately, or email first to ask if now is a good time to talk?

8. A colleague, applying to present at the same conference as you, repeatedly misspells the name of an important intellectual in

your field in her abstract. You are in direct competition for the limited travel funds made available to your department, but your colleague is established while you are still building a career. She also recently introduced herself to you at the faculty meeting you both attend monthly, four years after you first met her.

The quandary: Should you cancel class while you are at the conference, or leave a video for your TA to show?

I See You.

This is just to say that I see you. I know you think you are unnoticeable, but you're not. I saw your boots in the bathroom stall next to me, so I know you've been on the right floor for at least fifteen minutes. I noticed you slink in, arriving just as class began so you didn't have to talk to anyone. You took the last seat in the back of the room. You curled yourself over your phone, or laptop, or book. Your shoulders hunched and protected you. Your clothes draped so they hid you. But I see you.

You always do the assigned reading. From my desk, I can see your copy of the novel we're reading with your highlighting and scribbled notes. There's a Post-it on a page in the back—something you wanted to say, to point out, to make sure we discussed? I'll never know because you won't raise your hand, not even when I make a point to say that participation is expected, not even when I look directly at you, warmly but challenging, to indicate, "This is your moment! Speak up!"

Maybe this seems cruel to you. I keep trying to convey, but never seem to convince you, that I really want to hear your thoughts. That I really want your classmates to hear them too. Your written work excels. You have amazing insights. You answered the question I've posed, sure, but then you moved deeper into the topic, helping me see more than whatever I know about this story already. It's remarkable. You shouldn't keep that intellect to yourself.

You stopped by my office hours, a little nervous but eager to talk about Adichie or Paley or Fey or whomever we read this week. You were awkward, but no worse than any other student. You were awkward, but I'm awkward too. You were awkward but only a freak of nature isn't at age nineteen. You were awkward, but it was really, truly fine. But on the way out, you sort of slammed into the door frame, and you turned bright red, and that's it, I know you'll never stop by again.

When you stop coming to class, I try to find out why: emailing you, emailing your advisor, emailing a discreet classmate who I think might know what's up. You don't respond until I finally email that you should drop the class because you're sure to fail. "I'll be back next week!" you reply. You're not.

Eventually I have to stop trying and focus my attention on the students who do attend. One of your classmates has a sudden revelation about writing! It's great, but you mentioned the same idea to me in a paper you turned in weeks ago. You're not there, though, so I can't give you credit. I tell the student who's there how insightful she is, and she beams.

At the end of the semester the grade roster arrives, and I hope that I will see a W by your name, meaning that you withdrew. No. I have to type an F because you failed. I don't know if this F is the one that will pull your GPA down so far that you lose your scholarship or have to leave our school. Or maybe you've already left. Maybe you're at home. Maybe you're in a hospital. I have no idea. I know this is on you. But I can't help but feel I failed you.

I hope failing my class isn't a big tragedy for you. I hope it's just because you found something or someplace or someone you like better. I doubt it, but I hope. Anyway, I just wanted to let you know that I see you. I saw you. You were there.

An Incomplete List of Sources I Have Seen Plagiarized

The online menu of a steak restaurant in Chicago (I know this because the student included the phrase "Here at Chicago Steaktown, we value freshness . . ." in the paper, which I then googled.)

A rather famous poem by Robert Frost ("And I, I took the road fewer people took . . .")

Two students' papers, which they apparently wrote together in an elaborate but not well-planned double-blind con, hoping that by each blaming the other I would be unable to decide whom to punish and instead award them both passing grades (They both failed.)

An older brother's college application essay (She forgot to change the pronouns, and also didn't have much to say when asked about her topic: being her high school's starting quarterback.)

An article I wrote about teaching *Our Town*, which Mr. Amash must have found online because he made my points back to me, apparently without realizing it, when telling me how I should teach *Our Town*

This book (While I was working on it, a student who knew about it turned in a short story titled "Why Did I Get a C?")

Elizabeth Proctor's final scene in *The Crucible*

The Bible

I Know You're Asleep
Right Now, but Please
Get Back to Me ASAP

The Carnegie Museums of Art and Natural History sit right across the street from the Cathedral of Learning, Pitt's best-known building, which the students call Cathy. When I taught Seminar in Composition in Cathy, I always set aside a class meeting to visit the museums, because it's good to get out of the classroom, and besides, I wanted those freshmen to be aware that these outstanding museums were so close by, and free to them to boot.

Once, a giant rainstorm rolled across Pittsburgh on the late-October day I selected for our trip, so my students blew into the museums' foyer shaking water off their umbrellas and raincoats. One student, who I will call Pete, arrived late, after I'd already sent the rest of the class off to explore and write. Pete wore a T-shirt, cutoff sweatpants, and flip-flops. He was soaked to the skin and clearly freezing, but refused my suggestion that he go home and change into something warm and dry, since he could come back at another time at no charge.

"Nah, I'm good," he said.

"You could get sick, though," I said. "Do you have an umbrella?"

"Somewhere," he replied, waving vaguely. "My mom gave me one."

And then he squelched off to look at the art.

A week later, Pete didn't come to class. And then he didn't come to the next one. I was just about to remind him that he was nearly out of unexcused absences when I received an email explaining that Pete had contracted pneumonia, so he would be out for another week.

When Pete returned, it was almost the end of the semester. He'd lost weight and looked awful, a bundle of wiry anxiety and stress. I noticed, too, that he was now dressed appropriately for the weather, although I kept myself from commenting on this. But he said, "I should have listened to you."

"Oh, well, I doubt—" I began.

Pete shook his head. "I thought I was an adult," he said. "But . . ."

Neither of us finished his thought, but we both knew: he wasn't.

Pete and I didn't cross paths again, so I can't comment on how he changed from his freshman year to his senior, but I bet it was quite dramatic. Watching my students mature is one of the delights of teaching at the college level; somehow, over those four years, kids grow up into adults. That's not to say I've never had an extremely mature freshman in class. There are far more of them than there are extremely immature seniors, actually. Perhaps extremely immature students don't make it far enough to be seniors at Pitt.

Anyway, I'd guess every student grows up quite a bit from year one to year four, or to year five, or to, you know, a couple of years off and then back to year three. However it works out for them. I don't judge. Better to take three years or two decades off and then get a degree you've enjoyed earning in a major you feel passionately about than to bang through three and a half years and wonder why, exactly, you were so hell-bent on getting your premed degree, or realize that the only career you've trained for is going to be handed over to a robot in 2030.

Many first-year students enter with a vague idea about what they'll major in, ideas that come crashing down around them as the semester winds on like air conditioners falling off a high-rise in Brooklyn. I mean, if all my freshman students who started off intending to major in neuroscience actually did, we would have artificial brains by now. Instead, reality sinks in, that it's actually quite hard to be a doctor, or lawyer, or scientist of any kind, and that getting As from your high school's extremely engaging science department does not mean you're ready for Human Physiology, taught at 8 A.M. by a man with a strong accent who will not speak loudly enough to be heard by his class of two hundred. There's a reason why Pitt doesn't want freshmen to declare majors.

So, they live and learn. I think this is okay. And I like the flip side of this problem, which is when students arrive at my class sure that they hate English or reading/writing/the very alphabet itself, but through the joy of having it taught in a warm and challenging way, realize that they actually do like all of those things quite a bit. In short, there's no limit to the things eighteen-year-olds can be wrong about, bless their hearts. I can't tell you how often a student tells me at the end of the semester, "I thought I knew everything about writing already. I was wrong."

My experience teaching at the secondary level, as well as hearing about my students' experiences there, has convinced me that American high schools are often not actively helping students mature. This is one of the reasons I feel every high school commencement speaker should title her speech "Gird Your Loins, Youths, Here Comes Life!" When teenagers believe that they have reached the pinnacle of their lives at prom and high school graduation, it only makes their journey in college more of a climb.

But eventually they get there! Mostly! And watching that process is truly a joy as well as—if I'm being honest—often hilarious. I mean, it would not have been funny if Pete had died of pneumonia, but he didn't, thankfully, and the contrast between his moist bravado at the museum and his muted sadder-but-wiser appearance weeks later was a delight. Thank goodness he had that comeuppance. He needed to learn.

At eighteen I needed to learn, too, so very many things before I grew up. Here's one example: When I was in college, I drove an old clunker of a Chevy. One time, in the parking lot by my dorm, I decided that I was too tired (?) to back up (??) and instead tried to drive *over* the little concrete strip that separated one spot from another. (No, I was neither drunk nor high.) Of course, my car was immediately stuck, balanced like a seesaw on the concrete, and I ended up having to call AAA to come lift the car off the barrier, which, as you might have guessed, took a lot more of my precious energy than just backing out of the spot would have done. I particularly remember the AAA guy openly laughing at me. I couldn't blame him. Before I drove onto the strip, I remember thinking, "Why don't people just do this instead of backing up?" as if I alone had thought of the concept of driving forward. As my car wobbled there, stuck, I thought, "Ah. This is why." This is eighteen.

Like Pete's pneumonia, like my seesawing Chevy, college students need "Ah. This is why" moments. It's a pleasure and a privilege to watch them have them, to keep myself from laughing, to try hard to help, and to head home singing "I'm Glad I'm Not Young Anymore" from *Gigi*.

Observing them figure out how to communicate with fellow adults is one particular pleasure of mine, with email a special joy. The vast majority of students start at what I'll call the School of Extreme Formality. I've gotten emails addressed to "Dear Madame" and "Respected Miss." These notes tend to apologize for their existence and then lay out the student's entire career thus far before asking a very simple question, such as what our room number is.

I enjoy those, because I'd far prefer someone try too hard than not hard enough, as with those students who go in the other direction, the School of Trying to Be Cool. "Shannon," these begin, even if the student has not met me and thus doesn't know I prefer to be addressed as "Madame." Or they'll start with "S:" as if we are long-standing best friends. Or "Hey," which always makes me feel like the student is Joey Tribbiani and I am a comely guest star with one line on *Friends*. I am at the age where I appreciate everyone pretending I'm younger than I am, but come on! Class it up a bit.

Sometimes students attempt to use business-speak in communicating with me, particularly when arguing about a grade. Suddenly words like "negotiate" and "impactful" appear. I once had a student who had fairly earned a C in the class ask me if I could "work with" him on that grade. "Meet me halfway," he said, which bemused me. Was he asking for, like, a B Nearly +?

Email can also reveal a gigantic misunderstanding of my role in my students' lives, the kind of mistake that (generally) only freshmen make, and which I gently correct. They might ask me to print out or even photocopy their work for them (no) or send them my study guides (as I don't give tests, I don't have study guides, so . . . no). I used to get asked a lot for rubrics about how I will grade an assignment, which was particularly galling since my syllabus has a long section on how I grade, possibly the least-read work of literature since the other stories besides "The Dead" in *Dubliners*. To counter all of this, when teaching first-year students, I gave a short speech I called "I Am Not Your Secretary or Your Mom." At one point, I waved my hand around my face and said, "I know I'm round and female and nice, but still, I don't work for you!"

Most of them got it, but some did not. I don't blame them: high school and society have conspired together to teach them that women are there to help, especially if they, like me, have the face of a person who might like to give you directions. One time a student requested that I send him the PowerPoint of my lecture, a curious request I could not fulfill because I rarely use PowerPoint and my lecture notes consist of brief reminders like "Point of View" and "O'Connor/Gothic"—plus I rarely lecture for more than ten minutes. Another student emailed to say that she would stop by my office that afternoon so I could explain what she had missed in class that morning, unaware that my office hours would not be for three more days. She was quite annoyed with me in her follow-up email. First-year students have not yet learned that many professors are not in their campus offices from nine to five every day. And I cannot tell you how often a student who wasn't in class expects me to somehow re-create the two-plus hours they missed; I guess I'm supposed to use sock puppets to stand in for their classmates when recounting our intense once-in-a-lifetime discussion.

Outside of email, students ask me to diagnose their illnesses, explain how to use their laptops to them, and to recommend good restaurants in Pittsburgh and New York. I don't mind any of these things, really, although I absolutely refuse to do the first two and try to convey that Pitt is such a large university that we have better resources for them to turn to, like the Student Health Service and the twenty-four-seven IT Help Desk. As for the third, in Pittsburgh, I like Max's Allegheny Tavern, and in Brooklyn, Speedy Romeo pizzeria.

The push/pull between what students want me to do and what I am actually going to do can be intense, and sometimes grows hostile. I had a student who very much wanted me to counsel her about the difficulties she was having as a first-year student. I met with her several times and gave her my best advice about how to make friends, before concluding that she likely needed to see someone with better mental health care training (I gave her the information to do so) and that she was substituting these interactions with me for the peer friendships she needed to develop. She kept coming to my office anyway, and once I sat silently in the dark waiting for her to leave my door instead of allowing her to engage with me this way. Although my gentle redirection was ultimately what was best for her, she didn't think so, as she told me and my bosses on her evaluation of me that semester. "Shannon kept turning the conversation back to the work of the class!" she wrote. Imagine this in other contexts: "The lawyer only wanted to talk about the case!" "My doctor was fixated on my illness!"

I don't know a single professor who feels their absence policy works beautifully—even though Pitt lets us set our own—except maybe those who have given up trying to enforce one. I loathe dealing with attendance, and must constantly remind myself that it's good for the students to know that I'm tracking whether they're in class or not. I find it ridiculous to stand in front of a room full of adults and audit their presence. But hey, it's for their own good. (And, not for nothing, I'm told by students that they prefer an enforced absence policy than none at all, because it makes them feel, in the best possible way, seen.) I was a student who rarely skipped class, but I grew to hate those classes in which the majority of students didn't show up because they knew the professor didn't take attendance. I felt like a fool. So I persist in making little check marks in little boxes on my roster.

I once had a student miss four classes for no particular reason, as he himself told me. I warned him after absences two and three, but he missed another one without an excuse, so according to my syllabus, he had failed. As he had shown little effort in the work, which he often turned in late, I didn't much feel like giving him a way out of his predicament. I eventually gave him the opportunity to make up some work so that he could pass, on the advice of a colleague who'd been teaching at Pitt for longer than me, but I almost lost it when he offered to come to my house so I could (I guess) oversee him doing his homework. Uh, no.

On the flip side, after I returned to teaching following my father's death, one of my students stopped by after class to let me know that he would be happy to help me with various household tasks, like plumbing and woodworking, since my dad wasn't around anymore to do that. My father never held a hammer in his life, and I lived in an apartment at the time, but I appreciated his gesture so much. He had known me for two weeks.

His offer was innocent, but most professors are used to having a student or two crush on them every semester. I was lucky that by the time I got to Pitt I was more than fifteen years older than most students, and thus didn't endure too much of that. My TA colleagues who were in their twenties had a rougher time. But no one can avoid the cloud of hormones on a college campus. I carry a backpack to work, and usually wear jeans and a T-shirt or sweater, so I have had the occasional undergrad try to hit on me as they hold the door for me on our way into Cathy. The horror on their faces as I pass by and they realize I am a professor is reason enough to stick with this career.

I have a soft spot for the artists-to-be, as I was once one myself, and while I hold firmly to the belief that the art I created in my early twenties was quite good, it wasn't. I remind myself of that as I read my students' attempts to create meaningful work, knowing that while these students may not become great artists, this *is* how all great art begins. Once, I spent twenty minutes flipping through a student's portfolio of some of the worst fashion drawings I've ever seen, all the while saying things like "Ooh, so bright!" and "This one is eye-catching!" and "For the right person, wow!" They, like me, will soon enough learn that their youthful work was not world changing. Maybe they'll be kind to the young artists they meet too.

Sometimes students don't have time to create much, though. Instead, they're barreling through too many credits at a crazed rate, often realizing too late that they've taken on more than they can handle. The moments of panic that result are also moments of learning: every semester I get an email from a student (and often not a first-year student) that arrives after 10 P.M. even though they know that by then I have turned off my phone and likely am, as per my syllabus, "sleeping the untroubled sleep of a happy baby." These emails often read something like "Shannon I know that you're asleep and you aren't going to read this right now but just in case you're up for some reason anyway I'm having trouble with my story and I know you said we should have started working on it earlier but I didn't and now I'm remembering that you said that if we really, really, really felt stuck not to panic but to just email you and ask for a little extra time that it was better to do that than to freak completely out because the world isn't going to end just because I blew a deadline but at the same time I understand that I have to take responsibility for my actions and so that's what I'm doing asking for the extra time and also taking responsibility and I know I should have asked sooner but hey I learned that now and I won't make that mistake again thank you so much please get back to me when you're up."

When I write back, I tell them that they really did learn something, so good for them! And that they can have twenty-four hours to finish their story. Everyone makes mistakes, I say to almost every student over the course of the semester, and then have the joy of cutting them a break.

It's part of why I love teaching at the college level so much, not just that I can expect so much of my students, but that I can help them learn to navigate the trickiness of being an adult. I mean, as best I can. Let's be honest here: it's not like I have adulthood all figured out. Sometimes I look at my students who have color-coded planners and belong to thirty different clubs, who work full-time, doing a triple major AND an internship to boot, and I feel like a slacker. Maybe they just take more Adderall than me (which is to say, any Adderall) but I doubt it. They're just more together than I was at twenty. They'll be running the UN by the time they're my age, whereas I am applauding myself for remembering to fill up the windshield wiper fluid in my car.

Yet I'm also aware that my students struggle with anxiety in a way that my generation did not, at least not so openly and widely. The drive to be perfect is often tied to that anxiety. It's very often true that harmful mental processes are the foundation garment to whatever behavior my student is displaying, even good ol' Pete and his bravado—maybe he came to the museum that way because he didn't know how to act and so put off arriving until the last minute. Who knows? I doubt that even he did. Yet my students cannot go through life without stress, desire, passion, just because those emotions trigger their anxiety. Learning how to cope with rejection of and lack of interest in your most precious work is part of being a writer, and it's a skill set that serves them well in many other fields too. So I try to help them acknowledge, root out, and possibly seek help for their anxiety without letting it win, all the while thankful that they seem to feel they can be more open than I was about the panic attacks I experienced when I was younger.

I often think of that saying about being kind to everyone because you don't know what battle they're fighting today. Except for the kid who wants to argue about his grade, yes. I try to keep myself on the same side of the battle as my students and to look for ways to support their growth instead of becoming another force aligned against them. Most of the time I, a Respected Miss, succeed. And when I don't, there's always the joy of shutting down ye olde email at 10 P.M. and crawling into bed to get the eight-ish hours of sleep I know help with my own anxiety. I generally sleep well. I have faith in the kids who are out there, awake, keeping watch by night.

Sports Analogies for Academics

"Dude's a trash talker." = Dr. Smith never, ever holds the door open for anyone when leaving the faculty meeting at the same time.

"We've reached the two-minute warning." = It's the week before the conference you agreed to attend but haven't written the paper for yet.

"We won the Super Bowl! We're going to Disney World!" = Guess what? Your panel is canceled because everyone else on it didn't write their papers and bailed at the last minute! Enjoy your five pointless days in Des Moines!

"That guy's the heart and soul of our team." = He teaches only one class for ten students every fifth semester, but the department has been trading on his fame for years.

"It is what it is." = Ibid.

"This team is a family." = The long-dead subject of my dissertation is as close to a best friend as I have.

"It's the bottom of the ninth, bases loaded, full count . . ." = Hi, I'm the new vice provost for faculty innovation, and I'd love to hear your ideas for how we can improve!

"Do you believe in miracles?!" = No one seemed to notice that I used the made-up word "panopticonitical" in a committee meeting.

"We're looking to bring in some fresh new talent." = We have $15,000 left over so we can hire five more adjuncts.

"We're taking it one game at a time." = I just have to live with the fact that I told my class that *Pride and Prejudice* is my favorite novel on the first day.

"She plays an intellectual game." = She sprinkles in references to the Sweet Valley High books in her papers.

"He's not a great athlete but he's a good locker room guy!" = He never has much to say in committee meetings, but he does always bring Trader Joe's Dark Chocolate Peanut Butter Cups to them.

"She's a real student of the game." = She is the one student in my Comp 101 section who seems to do the reading every time.

"Hall-of-Fame-level performance!" = They were almost on *CBS This Morning* but got cut because of breaking news.

"We always give 110 percent." = We always give 85 percent.

"He left it all on the field." = He broke down sobbing after his dissertation defense.

"It's a rebuilding season." = We hosted the biggest conference of our field last year, and thus we do not need to do anything more until the late 2030s.

"Look, at the end of the day..." = Rebecca Solnit says...

"The other team just wanted it more." = The guy who got the job you went up for overworked himself into a hospitalization and can't teach for a full year.

"Get your head in the game." = Hit Send on that article submission already.

"Why Did I Get a B?":
An Answer in
Four Fables

Once there was a rabbit who was brash and bold, and perhaps just a little bit too likely to interrupt the wise old owl with what he said was a question but was really an observation, and he often did this just as she was about to make important points about *A Room of One's Own*. The brash rabbit worked hard, but not nearly as hard as some of the other rabbits in the class, which perhaps the brash rabbit did not realize because he was always talking so much, and once talked for so long past the end of class that he kept the wise old owl from catching her bus on time, so that she had to wait for an extra half hour in a Panera and ended up ordering one of those chocolate chipper cookies that tend to make owls gassy. At the end of the semester, the brash rabbit turned in a final portfolio that was fine and met all the requirements but also consistently spelled all forms of "there" as "theyre" and included a note explaining that he didn't have time to go back and change them all since he was more concerned with his "real" classes for his major in bio. The wise old owl gave the rabbit a "B"—which might stand for "brash"— but which also might just be what he earned.

———

One day, on their pilgrimage to the end of the semester, a monk and his apprentice came to a river.

"This river," said the monk, "is never the same twice."

"Well," the apprentice said, "actually, you mean that this river is never the same twice to us. Or, more precisely, you can't put your hand in the same river twice. My high school chemistry teacher, who was the best teacher I ever had because he came in at six A.M. to help me every day before practice, always said it like that."

A passing group of other monks and their apprentices tittered. The monk smiled at his student and said, "Thanks for correcting me in front of my friends. I can't tell you how grateful I am that you did that."

"Sure!" said the apprentice, who began to cross the river. "I just wanted you to know what the correct saying is."

The wise old monk smiled again. Then he pulled out his iPhone and sent himself a voice memo reminding himself to show his appreciation to his student at the end of the semester.

———

An elephant professor welcomed visits from her students on Tuesday afternoons from 3:00 to 4:50. One day she was visited by a mouse student at 4:45.

"I have so many questions about how to be an elephant!" the mouse squeaked.

"That's wonderful!" said the elephant. "I'm an expert on being an elephant!"

"Great," squeaked the mouse, "but before I ask you about being an elephant, can I tell you about the rough time I'm having with my roommate?"

"Oh dear," said the elephant. "Perhaps you should talk to the resident assistant mouse about that, or even just another mouse student."

"Yeah, I guess," said the mouse. "But I thought you could maybe help me because you're a girl elephant."

"Oh dear," said the elephant again. "I'm really so much better at just teaching you to be an elephant. That's my actual job."

"So," squeaked the mouse, "I've always been a heavy sleeper, even when I was just a little mouse with fifty brothers and sisters..."

"But it's 4:55 now," the elephant said, "and I have to teach at five!"

But the mouse didn't stop telling her story. In fact, she started to cry.

Like all elephants, the professor never forgot.

———

The princess was concerned about the lack of learning in her land, and she called for her ladies, telling them that the one who best presented what she had recently learned would be given a priceless treasure. One by one, the ladies shared their knowledge. The four most memorable were as follows: One lady wrote a complicated but beautiful poem comparing the orbit of the moon to a wolf making its way through the forest. The princess was fascinated. Another lady wrote an exquisite research paper on how airlines set prices, a topic that the princess was interested in but had never really read up on. A third lady wrote a short story based on the various uses of plutonium, yet another revelation to the princess. And a fourth lady made the princess this cute little hedgehog out of clay. The princess decided to give each of the first three ladies a priceless treasure, while the lady who made the hedgehog—which was totally cute but not that original, really—should receive a treasure that was not priceless but still expensive and rare. Unfortunately, the princess forgot the ladies' names and ended up giving the fourth one the priceless treasure that should have gone to the second one. Whoopsie! But it happens. There are a lot of ladies in that kingdom.

Taught

I: An Incomplete List of Things I've Heard People Say Should Be Taught in School

Manners

Morals

Ethics

The US Constitution (It is!)

The Bible (It can't be! At least, not the way this person meant)

How to balance a checkbook

How to check and change the oil in your car

How to negotiate a good price on a car

Whether to lease a new car or buy a used car (We're in need of an entire car curriculum, apparently.)

"The words to patriotic songs like Lee Greenwood's 'Proud to Be an American'"

How to apply to college

How to get a social security card

Fire safety

How to cook rice

How to cook pasta

How to cook anything, including a "good steak," over a fire so "the children are ready for the apocalypse"

Personal finance

The stock market

"The Internets"

Latin

The state capitals (pretty sure this is covered)

How to read a map (again, yes, done)

How to survive in the woods for weeks alone (Okay, you got us there—this is not covered.)

How to properly clean a toilet

Shoeshine skills

"Agricultural opportunities"

Basic common sense

The rules of American football

How to mix a martini

II: An Incomplete List of Things I've Taught My Students Beyond Our Curriculum

The words to the Black National Anthem "Lift Ev'ry Voice and Sing"

How to tie your shoelaces

How to swipe a MetroCard at a subway turnstile

What to do if you get on the uptown Q but the rest of the class gets on the downtown Q

The words to the unheralded American classic "Weiner Man"

How to attend a theatrical performance

How credit cards work (This is always a sad class.)

How to submit your work to a publication for consideration

How to find a college you might like to apply to

That you should at least visit that college before applying

That college is not at all like the *Pitch Perfect* movies portray it

How to bake a cake

Why you should not play Three-Card Monte at the Coney Island boardwalk

The "Thirty Days Hath September . . ." rhyme

That the moon doesn't leave the sky when it isn't visible

That Ireland doesn't have snakes

The difference between England, the UK, Great Britain, and the Commonwealth

Not to walk around while brushing your teeth and a haunting story as to why

What to do when there is no chalk in the room but you need to write something on the board

That it's "Flannery" not "Flattery" O'Connor

That going to counseling is a fine and healthy thing to do

That most problems can at least be mitigated by eating something, taking a walk, or taking a nap

That it's okay to like TV *and* books

The best writers read a lot, so if you don't like to read . . .

That whatever you love, there are other people out there who love that too

If you're not disabled now, you most likely will be at some point in your life (This is also not a happy class.)

That no one wants to read your *Buffy the Vampire Slayer* fan fiction, sorry

That there was once a book called *The Rules* and what those rules were about

That getting married/publishing a book/getting into grad school will not, by themselves, make you happy

III: An Incomplete List of Things My Students Have Taught Me

How to French tuck your shirt

What "bougie" means

At least forty more apps than any other person my age who doesn't
    work in tech knows

Grit

How to continue to live your life despite a chronic illness

That there's a cafeteria in the basement of the building I'd taught
    in for four years

What Pottermore is

Who Lana Del Rey is

The rules of American football

How Subway workers prep for the lunch rush

How to switch between accounts on Twitter

How to keep going even if you're the only one who thinks you can
    do it

How to cling to a foolish dream

How to abandon a foolish dream with relief

How to get from Rockaway to LaGuardia Airport by city bus

That it's harder than you think to hide that you're high

It's okay to cry in front of a class

It's okay to burst into laughter in front of a class

It's okay to be a little late if you couldn't find a parking spot, but
    don't make a habit of it

Every season, you should take the elevator up to the top of the Ca-
    thedral of Learning and check out the view of Pittsburgh from
    the top floor

The rules to competitive table tennis

Text your mom, if you can

What happens if you have a panic attack on a Swiss Alp

That the world of competitive Irish step dance is cutthroat

That the classes are long but the semesters are short

That someone is always listening

That they are onto me: the worksheets *are* just busywork

Everyone Who Attends
Must Converse

After nineteen years as a teacher, I can no longer shrug help-
lessly, pretending I don't know how I ended up in this career.
If I didn't especially want to become a teacher, and if, as I've chron-
icled here, I continued for reasons of expedience as well as passion,
I can at least end by saying that now, as I begin my twentieth year
of teaching and my third year of being full-time at Pitt, I have made
my peace with teaching. If you are what you do, then it is what I am.
Better, even: I often love being a teacher.

There are aspects of it that still grieve me: I hate that because
I'm a woman, I have to work harder to get people to believe I'm a
professor. I hate that I'm assumed to be a scolding prude, which
is deeply unfair: I am not a prude. I hate that even in the halls of
academia, there are folks who feel teachers should be nice but not
funny; hardworking but not ambitious; proud of their students but
not proud of their own accomplishments. I don't think I'll ever accept that some people simply will never believe I work hard enough
just because I won't meet them whenever they like, do whatever
extra work they want me to take on, or devote all my time to my
students. And I hate that so few of the students I teach will join me

in this deeply rewarding profession because they know they will never be paid enough to live the kind of lifestyle they'd like—a lifestyle, I hasten to add, that is not luxurious or decadent but that meets their needs and a bit more. Worse, for those who do want to join me in teaching at the college level, there may not be real jobs for them. And there are always semesters when my schedule is so wonky I am perpetually hungry or tired, and when my students seem to come in but two varieties: totally fine and PROBLEMATIC. But still, I love what I do.

This has a great deal to do with what I teach now—mostly creative writing classes, specifically in fiction and humor—as well as the students I teach, who are mostly smart, focused, hardworking, and a great deal of fun. We both want to be there, which is *the* key to making teaching a good job. I am particularly lucky to have found work teaching a subject that doesn't cease to interest me, and which I am still learning about myself. In fact, writing is so complex that I think I could spend the rest of my career teaching it and still discover new things, which, as you may recall, I did not feel while teaching the six canonical (and several improvised) verses of "The Wheels on the Bus."

I can also enjoy teaching because—and believe me, I write this with some trepidation—I have begun to feel a small sense of mastery of it. No, that's too strong. Do not smite me, Ye Gods of Education! I just mean that I often feel like I know what I'm doing. Mostly. Sometimes.

Don't get me wrong—I still feel slightly ill before almost every class. I still need to review any assigned reading before I teach it, no matter how often I've taught it before, which means I've likely read Faulkner's "Barn Burning" thirty times. (I don't know if you're familiar, so let me just say: that's too many times.) I have copies of texts with seven different colors of highlighting on them and a few different colors of pen ink underlining too, texts that I first read in the 1990s yet still don't feel entirely competent in teaching.

I still mess up on the regular. I forget my laptop converter for the SMART Board at least once a semester and my lesson plans at least twice (and when I do, like Eminem, f— that beat, I go a cappella). I pronounce so many words incorrectly, and never remember the phrase "free indirect discourse," which actually comes up quite a bit in the fiction-writing classroom. I don't pick up on bad mojo between classmates until someone is crying in my office. I still fail to realize what's most important to my students (correct pronouns, downtime, free snacks) and insult them accidentally. I know that there are students who really like me who are nonetheless doing homework for another class during mine. I have not yet managed to persuade students to put their phones away, like, entirely, really, fully away, for my class. I don't reach every student. I don't really love every student either, although I keep trying to. I have been accused, alas, of hating books. But I've gotten better.

To think about how that happened, that process of improving, is interesting. It was brutal at times, and even now I'm tempted to say that the lessons of some of the schools where I taught were entirely negative. But that's not fair to my students, who at every school have given me so much of their attention, time, friendship, and knowledge. I can see the legacy of every place I taught in my work today. From teaching at RLC, I learned about kindness, and the power of stopping for a rest and a snack (as I still advise my college students: 95 percent of the time, what they need is to sleep, to eat, or to go for a walk). From the fancy preschool, I learned that parents are scared, and that their fear trickles down into their students, and that money buys a lot, but not happiness. From teaching at Stella, I learned that love has a place in the classroom, even the classrooms o' the teens, and that being sincere is the best stance because it's true. From THSB, I learned that a few great colleagues/ friends can make a terrible job bearable. Also, that creativity and intellect don't limit themselves by skin color, but that assumptions and prejudices hold too many back. From being a grad student who taught at Pitt, I learned that people *need* to write—to express themselves, to learn about the world, to know who they are and what they care about, and that writing about teaching was a perfectly good subject. From my adjunct work, I learned that college students have deep, persistent anxiety, and allowing them to express that and learn to live with it is a noble goal. From teaching full-time at Pitt, I'm learning that creative writing isn't a garnish to a life of actual intellectual rigor but rather a full and glorious course of study to base a life on.

From everywhere, I learned that I might as well say the thing I'm thinking about the work we're doing, no matter how obvious or clichéd or cheesy I think it is: someone hasn't heard it before, and someone needs to hear it. I also learned that whatever is going on in the classroom is almost never about me, which I find surprising, humbling, and, eventually, obvious. I also learned that I must set my own boundaries, because people will take everything they can from a teacher and not even thank her lifeless husk of a body as they walk away with her lifeblood. Also—stickers! Everyone loves stickers!

Somewhere along the way, I picked up some magic tricks. I learned to sense time's passage so well that I rarely need to check my watch—I can almost always correctly guess what time it is in a class, and my students will tell you that I never keep them late, ever. I developed a series of jokes that always land, including my favorite:

to very seriously ask the students to take out a sheet of paper and put their name at the top. Then I wait ten seconds and say, "Ha, you thought this was a QUIZZZZZ! It's NOT!!!" (This *kills*.) I know exactly when in the semester to let the class out early. By dumping a bunch of boxes of cake mix and pudding into my stand mixer, I can bake a cake for my class that almost everyone loves but takes me only about fifteen minutes of work. I have developed a facial expression that is determinedly neutral but makes any guilty student immediately confess. I do accents in a pinch: my southern belle and British posh are particularly good, still.

I learned the trick—the gift, really—of being vulnerable, and relying on a bunch of people I don't know to help me navigate the class with my crappy hearing. This trick is self-perpetuating—now I feel comfortable being vulnerable enough to ask my students to work with me to create the class they'd like, a place where they'd learn best. I am a better teacher because I maintain authority but don't demand unquestioning obedience, nor feel that I must provide all of the answers. The authority is not about my ego but to protect the stated goal of our being there: to learn.

I learned grace: to apologize when I was wrong or gave offense, and to offer forgiveness when wronged. I say "Don't worry about it" and I mean it. I say "No big deal, we all make mistakes," and for a few short seconds, no one has ever made a mistake, we all have clean slates, and we walk in the sunshine of our perfect lives.

I learned that being dependable isn't dull at all, but a rare feat to be celebrated. I learned that George Saunders, Kate Atkinson, and Chimamanda Ngozi Adichie are wonderful writers and excellent to teach but tricky for some students to understand, while everyone loves Toni Bambara's "The Lesson" and Langston Hughes's "Theme for English B." Also, there are always students who dig Saunders,

Atkinson, and Adichie, and will praise my name for the rest of their days after they've been introduced to their work. I learned that there's a reason we still teach *The Crucible* and it's in John Proctor's final howl of self-awareness. I know that my students like it when I use words like "myriad" and "obviate" in casual conversation and that if I find a way to work in the last one, I get to tell the story of the student at Stella who used it this way in a sentence on a vocab test: "I obviate once a month."

I learned to make deadlines for the class and stick to them, unless it doesn't make sense to stick to them, and then to discuss it with the class before I change them. That letting them choose when something is due works fine. That there's really no need to force them into doing group work. That no matter how I extol participation, no matter how often I insist that they *must* converse, I cannot get everyone to participate in class. That the fact that I've been published in *BuzzFeed* means a great deal more to my students than credits for the *Paris Review*.

I learned that grief comes at you hard and fast, and it's not wrong to cry in front of your students. That when I teach the last act of *Our Town* I'd better bring in tissues, for me. That if I tell a student that his story made me cry, he'll start crying, and then I'll start crying again too, and then he'll cry harder. That it was fine to cancel class when we elected a sentient yam as president. That it was okay to email all my students to tell them I was thinking of them during the first Muslim ban outrage. That one of the students would email back, "Fuck you, TRUMP 2020!" and I'd be aghast, and then go on to teach him the next week anyway. He passed.

I have felt the crystalline pleasure at laughing with my students—of having a running joke with them, and dropping it into the class at juuuust the right moment. Of having a student make a joke at my expense that's so perfectly done, we all giggle for an hour after. Of letting them know that I know that they didn't do the reading, and that, while I'm not happy, it's also not the end of the world, so long as they repent.

I know to pack water for class, ice-cold, please, and that I can no longer justify wearing uncomfortable shoes. I know that I can go to the Panera on campus for dinner but not for lunch because the line is too long. I know that Pamela's has the best pancakes, but that I am well past the age when I could eat pancakes for lunch and then remain upright to teach later in the day. I know that the Pitt tech help department will always come to help me, even if it's the third day in a row I've called (Thank you, Shankir!). I know that the African Heritage Nationality Room in Cathy is terrible (hello, Africa isn't a country), but the Japanese Nationality Room is an aesthetic wonder. I know to check my fly before I teach. I know that if everyone is looking anywhere but at me, I forgot to check my fly. I know that in writing classrooms you open the blinds and let people daydream by looking at the sky.

There are still things I'm learning: How to help my students worry less about writer's block and trust revising more. How to make it clear that while I've worked hard to have my writing career, I've also been the darling of tremendous good fortune, and I cannot promise the same will be true for them, no matter how hard they work. How to stop saying "You guys" because it's offensive to my transgender and queer students. How to help that one student who is afraid of laughing to get over it. Why everyone loves Raymond Carver's "Cathedral" so much. Why overlooking multiple absences isn't actually a favor to them. Where on campus I can always find a parking spot. Why the kid who came to the first class left halfway through and never came back. How to grade faster, but not sloppier. How to stay interested in the three hundredth student story that's about a magical boarding school.

There's still so much to learn, to share, to listen to, to read, to teach. I love my four months of summer but I also can't wait to stand in front of the class and say, "Hi, I'm Shannon. We're going to have a great semester!" What I love the most is knowing that in the next classroom, another teacher is saying almost the same thing, maybe in a trembling voice, for the first time. And the next classroom down the hall has a professor entering her thirtieth year of teaching, her last, saying the same thing. And the next classroom down has a friend from my MFA days, greeting his class for the first time, and on and on and on, across Pitt, across Pittsburgh, across the country.

Year after year, we teachers show up, briefly putting aside our own lives for those minutes we're there, in order to improve, to help, to love. We're glad you're here, we say to our students. We're going to change you, you're going to change us. None of us will walk out of here the same. We don't even know how yet, but here we go. I love that feeling.

It's hard for me to remember that there was a time when I didn't love this job. It's there on the edges of my memory, conjured up in this book, but it feels remote, something that happened to someone else a long time ago. I'm so glad I didn't wait for the call from the burning shrub but instead trundled on into my life and found meaning in what I was given to do. It chills me to think of the students I wouldn't have met, the friends I wouldn't have made, the stories and essays I wouldn't have heard and read and edited and taught and written, were it not for this accidental, perfect career. What if my dad hadn't gotten me that job at the RLC, or if I hadn't figured out how to take the A train to Beach 112th? What if I had gotten off the B6 bus instead of going to that interview at THSB? What if I hadn't packed up the U-Haul with my things so that my brother could drive me from Brooklyn to Pittsburgh? I would have missed my life.

What luck, to stumble into a job like this one. So lucky, in fact, that it's almost like it was always who I was called to be. I am almost sure that I completely believe that.

Class dismissed.

Part IV

A Few Last Tidbits for the Cool Kids Who Like to Hang Out in My Room after School Is Out

My Last Pieces of Good Advice for New Teachers and Professors

Decide how you will take attendance and then stick to your plan, no matter how cumbersome it ends up feeling.

If you are really, truly stuck about what to do next in the classroom, ask the students to drag their chairs over to form a circle. That will give you at least three minutes, and possibly as many as ten, to come up with something.

If you really want to freak everyone out, carry a clipboard and walk around the classroom writing on it. It does not matter what you write. Frown a lot too.

I cannot overemphasize this: Never sit or place your foot on a desk in a way that propels your crotch area into your students' attention.

Do not say "we might get out early today" unless you absolutely intend to let them out early.

If you mess something up, fix it in a way that puts the onus back on you. For example, if I give students two due dates by mistake, I always make the assignment due on the later date. If they had that date in mind, it causes no problems. If they had the earlier date in mind, they just caught a break.

Let students turn work in early. You will be surprised at how much some of them really like this. It eases their anxiety.

A bag of candy fairly distributed on a cold winter's day can fix a lot of ills.

If you celebrate one birthday, you will have to celebrate *everyone's* birthday. (I do not celebrate birthdays in my classroom except with mild congratulatory praise because I cannot guarantee this level of togetherness.)

It's nice to tell the students you like teaching them, and to thank them for the hard work they put in for your class. I often comment on how great it is when, say, everyone turns in their work on time. I am also often told that I am the only professor who does this. I should not be. It took real effort from students. They deserve your thanks.

Ask before hugging.

At graduation, when you meet parents, tell them that their child was a complete delight and a joy to have in your classroom. Every single one.

How I Imagine Retirement from Teaching Will Be at Seventy-Two

A bright, not-too-hot April morning. The entirety of the University of Pittsburgh—faculty, staff, students—has gathered around a pedestal, where a statue is covered by a drape. Shannon, age seventy-two yet still beautiful and much thinner than she was at forty-five, enters, waving to the crowd.

The Crowd: (*chanting*) ShanNON! ShanNON!

Shannon: Oh, thank you, everyone! I am so delighted you could be here today! Let's give a warm round of applause to the ageless Sutton Foster and Bono for singing that beautiful medley of all my favorite songs.

The crowd applauds.

Shannon: Now I'd like to invite the president of the United States of America, who you know best as the student who told me she wanted to be like me when she grew up, to the stage to say a few words.

Jolene, a woman in her forties, takes the stage, hugs Shannon, and turns to the crowd.

Jolene: Okay, everyone, please take out a sheet of paper and put your name at the top. (*She waits.*) I'm just kidding! It's not a QUIZZZZ! (*Everyone laughs.*) A Shannon classic! Well, I'm just delighted to take time out from touring the country to see our completely saved environment to celebrate this special day with my dear friend and former professor, Shannon Reed. Sure, she's a PGOT—that's a Pulitzer, Grammy, Oscar, and Tony winner, you know—but this honor has got to mean a lot too, since it comes from the school where she's taught for so many years. It's time to unveil the first-ever artistic depiction of a non-tenure-stream faculty member on Pitt's campus! Here we go!

Together, Jolene and Shannon yank the curtain off the statue. It depicts Shannon at the front of a classroom, making finger guns and winking. Applause is robust at first, then dwindles.

Jolene: Oh! Huh.
Shannon: Oh.
Jolene: Well . . .
Shannon: Okay, sure. I mean . . . sure.

A silence.

Shannon: Are we . . . are we still doing the scholarship thing, though? For funny, young female-identifying writers? The one that's named after my Mum-mum?
Jolene: Oh, for sure. Tina Fey just texted me that she and Amy Poehler are on their way in for the big reading for that tonight.
Shannon: And we're definitely still doing the scholarship for young

African American men to go to college or trade school? The one that's named after my parents and Stan?

Jolene: Yep, yep. That's still on, and your mom will be there, ninety-eight years young!

Shannon: And we're staging that celebrity reading of *Our Town*, in which I get to play the Stage Manager?

Jolene: Uh-huh! And your closest friends are in it too! Andrew is backstage talking to Benny Cumberbatch right now!

Shannon: Okay, well, then it seems churlish to complain about the statue. Although I'm not really a finger-guns kind of gal.

Jolene: Yeah. Well, you know what? You probably won't even remember it's a whole thing by the time you get to your house in the Irish countryside.

Shannon: True...

Jolene: And hey, between you and me, you're up for the first-ever Kennedy Center Honors award for teaching, like, really performatively.

Shannon: Statue? What statue!?! (*She turns back to the crowd.*) Okay, everyone, let's get this dance party started! We have the B-52s! We have a hologram of Neil Diamond! We do not have the Electric Slide! There's pizza and shave ice and cake! The fountain on the quad has been transformed into a *chocolate* fountain! There's a crafting booth and lots of book-themed temporary tattoos! And don't forget about the introverts comfort area in the Texas Nationality Room!

Jolene: Happy retirement, Shannon!

Shannon: Thank you, Jolene! And thank you for representing all of my beloved students!

Jolene: No problem!

"Groove Is in the Heart" kicks off, and everyone, but everyone, gets down.

THE END

Acknowledgments

It would be a crime punishable by stoning—and I always try to avoid "The Lottery"-esque scenarios—not to begin my acknowledgments by thanking my students, past and present. I wish I could tell you more than I have here about them, dear readers. They are my constant delight, and also my constant aggravation, especially when they ask me something that they know full well is covered in the syllabus. Truly, I would not be a teacher if I didn't have the pleasure of their wit, intelligence, humor, compassion, empathy, righteous anger, and desire to grow. I'm aware of both the honor and the privilege of telling you some of their stories, and I hope that you will be able to read the stories *they* tell about their lives in their own voices someday soon.

Dear students: Although you know that my math skills are as terrible as my ability to draw anything on the board, I calculate that I've taught over two thousand of you in my career. I just don't have the pages to name each of you, so instead I'll thank you collectively: whether you're still a part of my life fifteen years later or vanished from my consciousness after a single semester, please know that you have changed me for the better. I've loved reading your words, hearing your thoughts, talking with you, and learning from you. It has been a pleasure and an honor to have played a small part in your education. Thank you, from the top, middle, and bottom of my heart.

I would be remiss if I didn't mention several specific students for profoundly impacting me, possibly in ways they never realized: thank you to Tyler K., Kathleen Monahan, Janelle Greenholtz Perez (best book ever?), Michelle Corvino, Ashley Gleason, Erica Dimanche, Nancy Cantalino, Becky Becvar, Arielle Lewis, Ariel Scotti, Tyronickah Buckmire, Jared Findlay, Aria Noel, Markus Martinez, Audrey, Meadow Fallon-Dora, Rebekah Miller, Tritan Plute, Claire Akers, the one and only Critter, Anna Monnett, Sonya Acharya, Doug Remmick, Amanda Schwarz, Nina Auslander, Johnny Ray, and Jake Schermansky. Special thanks and much love to the room 312 portion of Stella's class of 2008. I am also particularly grateful to all of the students in the fall 2019 Senior Seminar in Writing Fiction at Pitt, who cheerfully put up with me while I tried to teach *and* edit this book, and especially to Grace MacGuiness, Amanda Kotze, Anna Maria Hervey, and Laura Condon for being particularly supportive. Thank you, and whenever any of you ponder verb tense, may you think of me.

Love goes out also to Shakiyl, Shakiyla, and Mary. No teacher wants to outlive her students. I'm so sorry I did, and I think of you often. Your memory is a blessing.

Thank you also to my many colleagues over the years. Before I became a teacher, I didn't understand why teachers always hung out together, even outside of school, and thought it was profoundly weird. Now I understand that we do because no one else is off all summer, and also because no one else understands. Seriously, though, teacher friends are the absolute best: fierce, loyal, vibrant, and very quick to take your side. I've been so lucky to have many amazing teacher friends, some of whom are mentioned in this book, but I'll specifically thank a few: Mahalo to Danielle Duffy and Erica Giglio-Pac, sisters of my heart forever, who unflinchingly stood by me in my darkest teaching days. Thank you also to Liz Conte, my faithful Stella friend, and Aimee and Andrea, the best co-teachers I've ever had. I'm especially grateful to Kelli Buck and Andrew Gallagher for being very bright lights during a very dark time. My thanks to Rachel Bello, Elizabeth Heisner, and Natalia Ortega-Brown—although I've never taught in the same school as any of you, I know that you all exemplify good teaching. There wasn't room to write much about the many teaching theatre artists I worked with at THSB, and thus talented folks like Linda Key and JM Rossi didn't get mentioned when they were very much a part of making the school and my class shine. I'll get to you in my next book.

Principals and administrators come in for a deserved beating in this book, but I want to especially thank Geri Martinez, Ann Cordes, and Sister Barbara at Stella Maris High School, who ran a wonderful school and were deeply kind to me.

I'd also like to thank the terrible principals I've had, who made me a stronger, better person and educator. I don't think that's what you meant to do, but that which did not kill me made me write a book.

I must spend a lengthy paragraph on the folks at the University of Pittsburgh. My experience at Pitt was an unusual one: I went from being an MFA student and TA there to an alumnus to adjunct faculty to a full-time professor in the program. On that journey, I've had the same folks as both my teachers and now my colleagues, which has given me the opportunity to see how dedicated, talented, and awesome they really are. My thanks especially to our writing program director, Peter Trachtenberg, and director of undergraduate studies, Jeff Oaks, who've been stalwart supporters of my work as both a teacher and a writer from the beginning; they understood that I found meaning in doing both, and never made me choose one over the other. Brilliant writers themselves, their support has meant so much to me. I'm particularly thankful to Peter for helping me develop the essay that became "Paulie" in a creative nonfiction workshop in 2015, and to my then classmates—especially Jen Bannon, Sara Button, and Rachel Wilkinson—for their good advice on it as well. Thank you in particular to my colleague and former professor Irina Reyn, who has the annoying habit of being a great teacher, a staunch supporter, and an excellent writer all at once, and to professor and writer Michael Meyer, who had dreams for me before I had them for myself and is an inspiring mentor and colleague. Thanks as well to the extraordinary Angie Cruz, the deeply kind Bill Lyschak, the always-got-your-back Geeta Kothari, the low-key-brilliant Anjali Sachdeva, the delightful Sarah Leavens (449 forever!), the ever-supportive and talented Barbara Edelman, the kind and smart Nancy Glazener, the chill genius Jeanne Marie Laskas, the ass-kickingly smart Siobhan Vivian, and the rest of the Pitt faculty. Thank you as well to the lovely Andrea Laurion and the staff of the English office, who put up with me when I breeze in with a thousand questions. Thanks to Heather Kresge for being our in-house photographer and for managing to take a good photo or two of me for this book. And thanks to the two chairs of the English program in the time I've been at Pitt, Don Bialtosky and Gayle Rogers, who are stalwart leaders and educators and have gone out of their way to do right by me and all their faculty. I'm also very grateful to my classmates at Pitt in the MFA program, especially Jen Bannon, Jennifer Howard, April Flynn, Sara Button, Rachel Wilkinson, Gavin Jenkins, Nour Naguib, Stephanie Wilson Rothfuss, and Cumi Ikeda for the insight, critique, and friendship.

(Also, consider applying to Pitt, searching high school juniors who like words—we're amazing!)

I'd also be remiss if I didn't thank the staff and campers at Camp

Sequanota and Camp Ballibay, the two summer camps I worked at over six years. I learned a great deal at both, and am so grateful for the people and places they brought into my life. They don't get a lot of space in this book—again, there will be another one, just hold on—but I started to become a teacher at them. My special thanks to Chelle Jelleff, the Jannone family, Carole-Ann Moench, Kate Russo, Gregg Bruce, Kara Bruce, Laurence Tallman, Avril Luongo, and the late Greg Wiese.

Turning now to the writing side of my career, I'm grateful for my brief foray into publishing from 2000 to 2002, which taught me quite a lot about people and books at a time when I needed to know both. Thank you to John Cerullo for being a great boss amid the chaos.

In 2011, I was accepted for a summer session at the Cullman Center Institute for Teachers at the New York Public Library, led by Maile Chapman and overseen by Sam Swope, gifted writers both. It's not hyperbole to say that that week changed my life. I knew after it that I wanted an MFA in Creative Writing, and that led me to Pitt and everything after. Thank you to the NYPL for that week.

I'm so grateful and, frankly, still gobsmacked that Chris Monks, genius editor of *McSweeney's Internet Tendency*, first gave my work a shot. My entire writing career is really a result of his having said yes to a long joke about *Our Town* in 2014. I hope he doesn't rue what he has wrought. Profuse thanks too to Emma Allen at the *New Yorker*, fierce defender of humor and granter of long-shot wishes, and the many other editors I've had the pleasure of working with. Had I known how amazing it would be to collaborate with these folks, I would have started my writing career much earlier, although they wouldn't have taken any of my early work because it all would have been jokes about R.E.M. They make my writing better, and I'm very grateful to them.

It's a wonderful time in history to be a lady humor writer. We're a fierce and loyal band, and I'm especially grateful to Kimberly Harrington, without whom this book would not exist. Also Caitlin Kunkel, Brooke Preston, Fiona Taylor, Bizzy Coy, Devorah Blachor, Julie Vick, and all of the rest of our virtual girl gang for their support and for raising my game every time they publish something new.

A huge thank-you to those organizations that have financially supported my writing in recent years: the Greater Pittsburgh Arts Council, The Pittsburgh Foundation, and The Heinz Foundation. I'm also grateful to have received support from the European Studies Center and the art department at Pitt.

I searched long and hard (and also occasionally weakly and ineptly) for an agent who would get me and my work, and have finally found the goal of my quest in Ryan Harbage, who is smart, kind, and funny, and always insists on paying for my meal. Thank you, Ryan, forever. He, in turn, led me to Trish Todd, who is wearying only in how often other people in the publishing world squeal at learning that she's my editor and then tell me about her many wonders. How right they are, and how lucky I am to have her as an editor! I'm devoted to her for her steady hand in steering this ship. Thanks too to her assistants Caitlin and Fiora, who constantly reminded me that communicating by email can be a delight if it involves book people. I'm also grateful to have gotten pros like Joanna Pinsker and Shida Carr as the publicists for this book, and for the hard work of Michael Gorman, Annette Szlachta-McGinn, and Jimmy Iacobelli. Simon & Schuster is lucky to have them, as am I.

In one of the more delightfully mystical ideas you'll come across in a Lutheran church, my faith believes that we can send love and thanks out to people of "every time and every place," so I'm going to thank my writing idol here: Thornton Wilder, thank you for "Saints and poets, maybe . . . they do some" and everything else you wrote. Thank you as well to the very-much-alive Tina Fey, George Saunders, Kate Atkinson, Anne Lamott, Bill Bryson, and Ann Patchett for the inspiration.

While I'm here, thank you to God for this life of mine, proof that You love us and want us to be happy. Don't let me forget to share. Thank you to the various churches I've attended over the years that this book covers, from Mt. Calvary Lutheran Church in Johnstown, Pennsylvania, to Saint Peter's Church in Manhattan, to Zion Lutheran Church and St. Andrew Lutheran Church in Pittsburgh. Thank you to Dr. Tom Taylor.

Finally, I must, of course, thank my friends and family. Thank you to my fierce Facebook tribe, friends so lovely that I'm willing to be on that bedeviled platform: Nancy Lindeberg, David Ruhf, Seth and Meg Reinick, Dawn Catteau, Susan Messina, Tracy Busch, Jennie Keplar, Jennifer Morgan Flory, John and Faith Dowgin, and so many more.

Thank you also to Alison Bell (sorry, it's always Alison, not Alice, to me, no matter how famous you get), to Victoria Libertore and Jen Koltun, to Gordon Cox and Ryan Migge, to Corey Lange, to Mark Snyder, to Suzie Agins, and to Casey Weaver, all of whom have believed in my work as a writer and a teacher for a very long time, and who showed up at a lot of not-very-good theatre in order to demonstrate that belief. I love you, Brooklyn Gang. Thank you to Magda Pescenye, who put her chips on me early on and never wavered on her bet. Thank you to Matt Lavine, who will want me to note that he was my prom date, just in case this book sells really well and I become famous. He's a gentleman and a scholar.

Thank you to the Stollers—Melissa, Eric, and Adam—for their love and support in Pittsburgh. Thank you to Paul Kruse, Christina Farrell, and my other teaching artist friends. Thank you to the good folks of the amazing City Theatre in Pittsburgh for keeping me employed as a teaching artist for so long, and especially to Kristin Link for her friendship and smarts. Thank you to other Pittsburgh pals, including Cara McClaine, Brett Sullivan Santry, and so many more.

Thank you to my aunties, Drs. Nedra Reed and Gladys Craig, for everything they've done to help and support me, a list too long to recount here but that starts with slipping me a fifty near Lincoln Center in late 1999 and goes on to include teaching me how to make pickles. Thank you also to my aunt Linda and uncle Pete for their excitement and enthusiasm for my career. I remember with love and admiration all that my grandparents, Henry and Violet Reed, taught me and am thankful.

Thank you to Gretel Kaltenbaugh, who has known me since I was eighteen years old and somehow hasn't gotten tired of me. She's okay. Thanks too to Mama and Papa K.

Thank you to the Swick/Ellington clan in South Carolina, from my dear friend Melissa and her husband, Robert, to my godkids Susan Faith and David to matriarch Sue Swick. I hope I've made this family of teachers and students proud!

Thank you to Christine, Avery, and Caden Marr, or, as I think of them, Teenie, Fairy Girl, and Little Buddy. You're my favorites. Thank you for sharing this dream with me, lo these many years. Teenie, the Witchita Asylum awaits.

I can't fully put into words how grateful I am to my best friend, Andrew Hansen, who always answers my cranky texts, will discuss fabric and yarn with me for hours, and never tells me that I've had enough cake. My belief in his wisdom is such that when he told me fifteen years ago that I ought to become a writer, I immediately did it. I go through life feeling sorry for people who haven't had a Roo in their lives since 1992. What would I do if I hadn't met you? I love you, Andrew, and I promise that someday, I will wang chung tonight.

My brother, Justin, has been my closest pal since he arrived to knock me off my only-child throne in 1981. I'm so lucky to have a brother who's smart, interesting, caring, and really funny, as well as supportive of my dreams, and who has kept me abreast of all Star Wars/LotR/Marvel developments. Thank you, Poopie, and thank you as well to my dear sister-in-law, Kate. I honk on my jazz tube for you both.

I miss our grandmother, Kathryn Zeger, and our dad, the Reverend Ronald Reed, every day, and I wish that they had lived to see this book, because they were both tremendously good teachers. The memory of their fierce love, passion for learning, and belief in the good of other people sustain me to this day.

Great teachers are wise, funny, kind, compassionate, caring, skeptical, a little demanding, and always ready to laugh with you. Lucky for me, Gloria Reed, my mom, is all of these things. I'm so grateful for the way she has always taken care of me, and I know her sustaining love is the one true advantage I've had all my life. Thank you, Mom. I love you so.

Finally, thank *you* for reading. You hold in your hands a dream come true, and I'm so glad you're sharing in it. Someone taught you to be able to read it. Please, if you can, go tell that teacher thank you.

Credits

Originally published on *McSweeney's Internet Tendency*

If People Talked to Other Professionals the Way They Talk to Teachers

Other Vehicular Styles of Parenting

The Unspoken Rules of the Teachers' Lounge

Student Essay Checklist

I'm Going to Make It through the Last Faculty Meeting of the Year
    by "Yes, and ..."-ing It

If Bruce Springsteen Wrote about Adjuncts

Classic College Movies Updated for the Adjunct Era

Sports Analogies for Academics

"Why Did I Get a B?" An Answer in Four Fables

Originally published on NewYorker.com

Middle School Parent-Teacher Conference Night, in Internet Headlines